The Question is the Answer
To Enhancing Agile Project Performance

Printed in the United States of America.
First printing

ISBN-13: 978-1466286344
ISBN-10: 1466286342

1

Additional Titles By The Author

Take Charge of Your Own Development

Take Charge of Your Teams Development

The Question is the Answer:
500 Questions to Enhance Your Competitive, Moral, Social, and Emotional Intelligence

The Question is the Answer: Leveraging Questions to Enhance PMI Project Performance

The Question is the Answer: Leveraging Questions to Enhance PRINCE2 Project Performance

The Question is the Answer: Leveraging Questions to Enhance Project Risk Management

Notice

The material contained in this volume is intended for informational purposes only. The author disclaims liability for any personal injury, consequential or compensatory, directly or indirectly resulting from the publication, use, application, or reliance on the material in this publication. The author disclaims and makes no guarantee or warranty, expressed or implied, as to the accuracy and completeness of any information contained in this volume, and disclaims and makes no warranty that the information in this document will fulfill any of the reader or users specific or particular purposes, needs, or uses.

In making this material available the author is not undertaking to render professional guidance or any other service. The reader or anyone accessing this material should defer to and rely on their personal experience and independent judgment as appropriate as well as seeking the advice of competent, qualified professionals in determining how to apply the information contained in this volume.

Contents

Introduction

Introduction

There are several business books on the market today. They span the gamut of subjects, from how to lead and manage more effectively to how to make better decisions.

The characteristic common to most of these books is they offer advice, provide a plan, or recommend an approach. Whether it is "10 Rules to Better Business Performance" or "30 Days to Becoming a More Effective Manager", they seek to offer a specific approach, recommendation, plan, or solution to enable the reader to achieve a specific outcome.

Now make no mistake, I have read many of them and even have several of them in my personal library. Several of them are excellent in that they provide a specific set of ideas, insights, and recommendations. In that regard, they are excellent as a starting point. However, I believe their strength can also become their weakness. This happens because taking the advice of others can sometimes keep us locked into a lower level of learning.

In the 1950's educational researcher, Dr. Benjamin Bloom, identified six levels of cognitive or intellectual learning. Understanding these levels gives perspective on how specific recommendations or perspectives can sometimes lock us into that lower level of understanding, when in fact a higher level is needed and available. Let's look at each of these levels.

Bloom characterized the first three levels of cognitive learning as Knowledge, Comprehension and Application. Knowledge level learning is characterized by basic memorization. For example, the ability to recite the alphabet from A to Z is an example of this first level of learning. The second level, Comprehension, is present when wear are able to present the information back in the same manner and form in which we originally learned it. We see this level of learning present when a child is first learning the alphabet and they are able to name a specific letter when someone points to it. The third level of learning, Application, is present when we are able to take what was learned and use it in a form that is different than it was originally learned. A child who is able to take a box of blocks with the each letter of the alphabet embossed on them and arrange them in proper sequence is demonstrating application level learning.

The goal of many business, leadership and management texts is to get us to the comprehension or at best the application level of understanding. For example, take a book on the topic of quality service delivery. The material will start by defining basic ideas and concepts. This addresses the knowledge level. Next, the material provides examples of how the concepts and principles work. Case studies or personal examples based on the author's experiences or interviews with others are used for this purpose. This addresses the comprehension level. The author then encourages us to get out and use the material to improve our personal and professional practice and performance. The idea here is that we will be able to relate to the examples and cases the author has provided in a powerful enough way to enable us to move into action in ways that suit our personal situations and circumstances. This is application level learning.

This is fine as far as it goes. However, keep in mind I mentioned that Bloom identified six levels of cognitive or intellectual learning. The challenge and the opportunity are to develop a method to move the learning into the top three levels.

Bloom's fourth level of cognitive learning is Analysis. Learning at this level is characterized by the ability to examine current ways we can use what we know as well as considering how we can improve upon it.

The fifth level of cognitive learning is Synthesis. At this level, we are able to generate new ideas, concepts, principles and even new knowledge based on what we know.

Bloom's sixth and final level of cognitive learning is Evaluation. Ability at this level is characterized by competence in taking everything that was learned at the previous levels and assessing it both quantitatively and quantitatively. It also involves being able to make and implement effective decisions and actions based on the evaluation. When we are at the top level of learning, we also demonstrate the ability to move easily and readily among all of the levels of learning within our specific domain of expertise.

This material is designed to enable you to move into those top levels of cognitive learning. It does so by asking you to ask yourself questions about your industry, your organization, your team and yourself. In addition to helping you move into those higher levels of learning it also allows you to own both the answers and the outcomes. The answers and solutions you come up with are uniquely yours.

Foundations

Opening Thoughts

Questions drive learning. Learning drives development. Development drives performance. Performance drives success. The advantage to using questions to drive learning, development and overall performance improvement is powerful. In addition to help drive learning further up the chain of cognitive learning, they also enable and sustain continuous learning. All a person needs to do to keep learning is to keep asking questions. Are you interested in learning something new? Ask the questions, do the research, consult with experts, and get the experience associated with and in support of answering those questions.

It has been said that all journeys begin with a first step. By analogy we can also say that all learning and subsequent improvement begins with a first question. Here are some to get us started.

Questions to Consider
1. What is the current state of project based client service delivery in your organization?
2. How can you use questions to improve overall project performance and project based client service delivery in your organization?
3. What type of questions should be asked and need to be asked?
4. Are they being asked today?
5. If not, why not?
6. What needs to happen organizationally and inter personally for them to start being asked?
7. What is being done with the information being gathered from the questions that are being asked?
8. What can and needs to be done to improve in this regard?

9. How would improving in this area affect your project execution and overall client service delivery?

My goal is to use questions to help you move through the process of understanding Agile project management and how you can leverage it to improve project based client service delivery in your organization. But first, let's explore the power of questions a bit more.

Socratic Thinking

"The unexamined life is not worth living"

The Greek philosopher Socrates lived more than 2500 years ago. He is remembered for espousing many principles that live on to this day. Principles relevant to our discussion include:

1. Self-awareness and understanding is the basis for authentic living.
2. We all have the responsibility to question "conventional wisdom" to verify the truth for ourselves.
3. There is a substantial risk when taking someone else's word for it or merely relying on tradition.
4. We all have moral and spiritual authority over our own "soul".
5. Free speech, open dissent and questioning of authority are not a threat to a healthy organization or society; they are essential to it and strong indicators of it.
6. The most productive and effective thinking is disciplined by logic and personal experience.
7. Human dignity mandates that we all participate in a constitutional form of governance and government.
8. A sound economy should have due respect for private property, markets that work, and individual initiative and enterprise.

Questions to Consider

1. How do these principles and ideas resonate with you personally?
2. What additional principles and ideas can you add to the lists that are important to you?
3. How do they resonate in your project team?
4. How do they resonate in your project organization?
5. What opportunities for improvement exist for you personally as well as within your team and organization in the context of these principles?
6. How would improving in these areas affect your ability to perform as well as that of your team and organization?
7. What type of return would change and improvement based on these principles have to deliver to make the effort worthwhile?

The Socratic Method

Put simply, Socrates asked questions, and he asked a lot of them. In the process of his conversations with others, he never provided his own insights, conclusions or positions. Instead, he used questions to prompt those he was speaking with to consider theirs. In the process, he would compel people to think much more deeply, to consider alternatives, and even make surprising insights and discoveries. Socrates applied his "method" to everything, from the nature of courage and wisdom to the causes behind the decay of organizations and societies.

Now make no mistake, Socrates ultimately paid a high price for his method. Questions and the insights they drive challenge people and in the process, they can threaten people and institutions. His method challenged Greek leadership and their belief in The Oracle for all decisions and wisdom that governed their society. For his willingness to challenge others to question conventional thinking this he was judged guilty and sentenced to death.

We as people, organizations, societies and nations have made at least some progress over the past 2500 years. However, even today there is still sometimes a price to be paid for asking questions. Questions can still stimulate contrarian thinking, bring the status quo into question, and threaten the centers of power and influence. If questions are doing those things, they are doing what they are intended to do!

Questions to Consider

1. When do you use questions?
2. How do you use them?
3. Why do you use them?
4. What do you do with the information and insight you gain from the questions?
5. What do those you ask questions of do with the information gained from the questions?
6. What opportunities for improvement exist in this regard?
7. How would improving in this area benefit you, your team, and your organization?
8. What type of benefit or return would you need to see to allow you to believe that the change and improvement was worth the effort?

Let's take this concept a bit further and apply it to the idea of self-examination.

Self Examination

Socrates believed people who do not know themselves and are carry self-deception about their own abilities are in the same position regardless of who or what they are dealing with. Be it working with people or institutions, the result will always be the same, one that misses the opportunity to be as effective as possible. His insight speaks to the idea that no one individual has all of the answers nor should they be expected to.

By no means was Socrates the only philosopher of his time. However, it was Socrates' ability to bring philosophy down to where he believed it lived, that being with the people that differentiated him from peers like Heraclitus and Anaxagoras. By doing this, he was the first of his time to apply and encourage others to apply critical thinking to the challenges they faced every day.

Socrates encouraged people to turn the lens of examination inward. He pressed the importance of relying on reason rather than revelation. Instead of people going to a Priest or The Oracle for guidance, he urged them to use their minds to understand themselves, their circumstances and their opportunities. As mentioned, he also encouraged people to question conventional wisdom and thinking. Socrates believed that for people to face the challenges they confronted every day without questioning their assumptions was done at their own peril. He encouraged people to start by examining their own intentions, values and capabilities. He believed questions enable people to get beyond easy and quick answers by showing them to be either contradictory or merely words that go now where and are meaningless. He used questions to engage people in the process.

Socrates would conduct these "dialogues" to enable people to see and understand themselves more clearly. His method also acknowledged the idea that people do not really begin to think until after they really hear what they are saying. When this happens, people begin to realize their beliefs and opinions are perhaps not as insightful or valid as they originally thought.

Questions to Consider

1. What is the "conventional wisdom" that governs the work you do in the area of project management?
2. What "conventional wisdom" governs the activities of your team and your organization in the area of project management?
3. Whom do you leverage as your mentors in this area?
4. What have you learned or developed the ability to do under their guidance?
5. What development opportunities are you currently focused on in the area of project management?
6. Why these specific ones?
7. What process or approach do you use to think through issues before making decisions regarding project management?
8. Who do you seek input from?
9. What criteria do you use to evaluate the quality of your decisions?
10. What is your preferred thinking style?
11. How can you use other thinking styles to improve your overall potential for performance and effectiveness in the area of project management?

12. What types of activities energize you?
13. What methods of self-reflection do you use to gain insight about your decisions and activities in the area of project management?
14. How do you leverage the insight you gain through self-reflection to improve your overall performance and effectiveness?
15. What types of questions do you ask? When do you ask them? Whom do you ask? How do you ask? What do you do with the answers and information you receive?
16. When do you challenge your own assumptions and those of others? How do you challenge and question your assumptions and those of others?
17. When have you not challenged your own assumptions or those of others, only to wish later that you had?
18. What prevented you from questioning at the time?
19. How do you enable yourself to objectively analyze and critique as well as sustain creativity?
20. What types of circumstances need to exist in order to enable you to question your opinions, attitudes, and beliefs?
21. What has to be present to enable you to change them?

The Socratic Method – An Example

Let's apply the discussion to an example. Start by thinking of and choosing a statement seen by many as self-evident or unquestionable.

Example – "Doing the right thing means standing by your values and never wavering or deviating from them."

Now, treat the statement as if it is false. In other words, "Doing the right thing does not mean always standing by your values in an unwavering or unshakeable manner." Put in the form of a question, "When might doing the right thing mean not standing by your values?" Then look for situations where your original statement is not true. When you find such exceptions or situations, you know you know your original definition is not adequate.

The original proposition now has to be modified to accommodate the exceptions or situations where it is not true or otherwise correct. A new, more accurate statement might read something like "Doing the right thing may require you to be able to stand by your values when appropriate as well as recognize and adjust to those situations that go contrary to your values and beliefs".

Continue the process by looking for other situations that clarify and support the new idea. Through the process of correcting inadequate concepts, beliefs and ideas you develop and strengthen your ability and willingness to develop a deeper and truer understanding of what you are really talking about and what you intend to convey through your thinking and communication.

Questions to Consider

1. What key experiences in your life have shaped your attitudes and values regarding project management?
2. What types of activities do you engage in to stimulate your thinking and enable you to generate new ideas?
3. How do you use open and close end questions?
4. What types of questions do you believe you need to be asking to enable you to most effectively pursue and achieve your goals?
5. What are the most important questions you believe you need to be asking?
6. To whom do you need to be asking these questions?
7. How do you enable and sustain the willingness on the part of the members of your team and organization to ask questions?
8. How do you use questions to stimulate the thinking and creativity of the members of your team and organization?
9. What can you learn from expert interviewers about how to ask the most effective questions?
10. How do you use questions to enhance the learning, development and performance of yourself as well as members of your team and organization?
11. What are the most powerful questions you can ask to enhance your effectiveness in any domain or area you chose?
12. How do you leverage these questions?
13. When do you leverage these questions?

14. How can you leverage the following ideas about questions to make the ones you ask as powerful as possible?

- ◦ They direct our focus.
- ◦ They direct our perception.
- ◦ They change the way we feel.
- ◦ They change our perception of and access to resources.
- ◦ They change our priorities.
- ◦ They change our understanding.
- ◦ They change our willingness to act

Getting to Application and Beyond

One very effective method of self-improvement is taking a problem and rephrasing it as it has already been solved. For example, self-examination phrased as a problem statement could be something to the effect of "How can I improve my ability to develop a deeper, more effective level of self-awareness?"

Now, take the problem statement and rephrase it as if has already been resolved. Taken this way it could read "In order to demonstrate a deeper level of self-awareness I will have had to have.....". You then identify each of the activities associated with achieving this state. Specific activities associated with achieving the ability to demonstrate a deeper level of self-awareness could include:

1. Developing a personal understanding and appreciation of the importance and value of a deep level of self-awareness.
2. Identifying key sources of feedback.
3. Calling on and requesting feedback from these people.
4. Leveraging the feedback in support of a better level of self-awareness.
5. Applying this enhanced level of self-awareness in my personal and professional relationships.
6. Soliciting and leveraging feedback to continue to enhance and reinforce the process.

By thinking though the opportunity in this way you are able to develop a specific improvement plan with supporting activities. With these ideas in mind let's move the discussion to focus even more precisely to thinking for ourselves.

Thinking for Ourselves

What is your reaction to the following statement, "Don't be convinced by me be convinced by the truth."

Socrates continually emphasized the importance of people doing their own thinking, the emphasis being on confirming or refuting what we have been told or what we have observed. He said this applies even when we are presented information from experts or well-known and respected sources. Ultimately, we are all responsible for judging for ourselves through logical examination and discussion with others.

For some this identifies the need and opportunity to develop a higher-level capability and competency. This competency involves the following:

1. You must see yourself as a thinker. Developing, demonstrating and refining your ability to think for yourself accomplish this. The greater the skill and ability the more you will trust in it, leverage it, and rely on it.
2. You must also develop your intuitive senses. Recognize when things, issues, or situations do not sit well with you. Recognize, accept and act on the idea that when something is not sitting well with you it is an opportunity for you to think more about it.
3. You must have and apply a strategy when considering and examining issues and problems. It can take whatever form works best for you, e.g., inductive, deductive, etc.

4. Understand when you have arrived at our achieved your own personal moment of insight. Then act on the insight.

Questions to Consider

1. Do you consider yourself a thinker in terms of being able to use your mind to the benefit of yourself and those that are important to you?
2. How open-minded are you?
3. How can you improve in this regard?
4. How do you continually challenge yourself to go beyond facts and into analysis, synthesis, and evaluation?
5. How do you ensure you are providing yourself with the opportunities to think through problems, questions, and issues that merit and require your attention?
6. How do you continually develop and enhance your ability to think linguistically, numerically, mathematically, chronologically, etc.?
7. What methods do you use to energize yourself and others to generate new and positive ideas and possibilities on issues, problems and opportunities?
8. How do you continue to develop and refine your thinking skills to adapt to constant change as well new and ever growing sources and access to information?
9. How do you continuously develop yourself as a scholar?
10. When looking at an issue how do you leverage an understanding of the positives and negatives as well as what is interesting about it?

11. How do you ensure you are aware of and considering all of the factors associated with an issue, problem, or opportunity?
12. How do address what will or might occur after a specific decision is made and put into action, to include benefits and consequences?
13. How do you integrate your goals and objectives into your thinking, analysis and decision making process?
14. When looking at a problem, issue or opportunity how do you identify and prioritize the most important factors to be considering, helping ensure key elements are addressed first?
15. How do you take the boundaries off your thinking to enable you to consider all possibilities?
16. How do you enable yourself to take another person's perspective or point of view on an issue, problem, or opportunity?

You may be thinking that I am encouraging you to challenge everything you know and have learned up to this point, as well as all that you may learn going forward. That's not the case. To explore this idea more in depth let's look at what "conventional thinking" is really all about.

Challenging Convention

"Conventional Thinking" is based on everything we both individually and collectively know (or think we know) up to a specific point in time. It is based on the accumulation of wisdom, knowledge, learning, and experience that characterizes who we are and what we know at a given point in time.

Conventional thinking and wisdom helps us deal with and manage the huge amounts of information we are presented with on a daily basis. We look at situations or issues, examine them for key indicators that align with our current understanding, analyze the issue in the context of our current knowledge, then decide and act based on what we know. Conventional wisdom is useful because it helps us deal with large amounts of information and make decisions quickly and for the most part effectively. However, it can also limit our ability to gain insight. It does this by either blinding us to new information or causing us to apply generalizations that are no longer accurate, are not relevant, or both. This is especially dangerous when it comes to managing project risk.

A good metaphor for a generalization is a "cave". When we enter a cave, we limit our path and destination to where the cave takes us. This is fine provided the destination is where we want and need to be. If it's not, it can create problems.

Socrates believed we are born in the "caves" of our mind. He believed that we ultimately stay there unless we make the effort to leave them. These "caves" represent what he refers to as our "received beliefs". We all carry a variety of values, attitudes, and opinions that we have absorbed based on our upbringing, education, culture, and socialization with others and through the media. We are bound to these ideas by our desire to please others, be accepted, and the desire to simplify our ever more complicated lives. Breaking out of these "caves" involves:

1. Visiting a "cave" from which we have already broken free.
2. Exploring the cave shared by a thought or opinion leader or someone whose opinions and perspectives are shared by others.
3. Explore some of the caves where pre-conceived ideas still live. For example:
   - "If it is worth doing, it is worth doing well".
   - "All that glitters is not gold".
   - "To the victor go the spoils".
   - "Better safe than sorry".
   - "Never burn a bridge; you might have to cross it again someday".
   - "If you can't say something nice don't say anything".

And once you have done these things:

1. Put one of your core most fundamental beliefs on trial for its very survival.
2. Cultivate skepticism as a core skill.
3. Use experts wisely.

Questions to Consider

1. What caves have you already broken free from?
2. How did you go about breaking free from them
3. What was the effect of your being able to break free?
4. How can you replicate this mindset and actions you used to break free from that cave to other situations you are facing?
5. What caves are you still living in?

One method we can use to break free from caves is to "speak the truth" to both ourselves and to others.

Speak the Truth

Socrates felt that commitment to the truth had three elements: personal, social and political. He felt it was important to confront individuals and institutions that were deluding themselves. Socrates believed people and institutions were guilty of self-delusion when they did not address social issues that merited scrutiny or political issues that were misunderstood.

Socrates believed organizations decay and rot from within, starting at the top, when they choose or are compelled to suppress or ignore criticism and deep examination. In retrospect dissent and the willingness to question "conventional wisdom" are seen as activities that would have saved the organization or entity. The willingness and ability to engage in these types of activities Socrates believed fulfilled the highest callings of organizational citizenship. The willingness to question conventional wisdom, to speak the truth, demonstrates the deepest level of caring.

Put another way, questioning the status quo is a responsibility. Feedback is a gift. If the person providing the feedback did not care about the person they were sharing the feedback with they would not say a word. They would simply let the person continue to do whatever they are doing, making whatever mistakes await, and suffer whatever consequences result.

Questions to Consider

1. How do you enable and sustain your willingness and ability to tell the truth to your family, friends, colleagues and team members, even when doing so is uncomfortable?
2. How could your team and organization improve if members felt more comfortable and were more willing to express their position, perspectives and questions more openly?
3. How do you determine if you are telling the truth as often as you should?
4. What type of personal test or standard do you use to decide whether to tell the truth?
5. How do you react when your organization, institution, or profession is engaged in activity that you know is deceptive, either to the public or to themselves?
6. What has compelled you to speak up when you have disagreed with what the majority was saying or advocating?
7. How do you work with others to advance the truth and act on it among your team, organization, and community?

Socrates believed that everyone has the responsibility to question what is going on. The goal of the questioning is to improve the situation, circumstance and outcome for everyone.

Summary

While the material did present some basic ideas and concepts, the larger goal was to engage your thinking in each of the areas. As mentioned, Dr. Benjamin Bloom identified six levels of cognitive or intellectual learning. Understanding these levels provides us with a perspective on how specific recommendations or ideas can sometimes lock us into a lower level of understanding, when in fact a higher level is needed. The goal is to get the highest level of understanding possible.

This material was designed to enable you to move into those top levels of cognitive learning. It did so by asking you to ask yourself questions about your industry, your organization, your teams and yourself. The goal was to enable you to move into those higher levels of learning. It also enables you to own both the answers and the outcomes. The answers and solutions you come up with are uniquely yours.

I hope that you agree the advantage to using questions to drive learning, development and overall performance improvement is powerful. In addition to help drive learning further up the chain, they also enable and sustain continuous learning. All a person needs to do to keep learning is to keep asking questions. Interested in learning something new? Ask the questions, do the research, consult with experts, and get the experience associated with and in support of answering those questions. What Socrates knew and applied more than 2500 years ago still resonates today. Questions drive learning. Learning drives performance. Performance drives success.

We started this portion of the discussion with some questions. Let's close in the same way:

Questions to Consider

1. How are you doing today?
2. How do you know how you are doing?
3. What are you doing to improve?
4. How do you know you are improving?
5. What are you doing to help others improve?

A Brief History of Project Management

A Brief History of Project Management

A project is defined as a set of activities performed to achieve a specific outcome within a specific amount of time using a specific set of resources. When looked at this way it is easy to see the results of project management across the millennia. Project management has been practiced since the earliest days of civilization. Consider the following examples:

The historian Herodotus (484 – ca. 425 BCE), and the scholar Callimachus of Cyrene (ca. 305 – 240 BCE) at the Museum of Alexandria, made early lists of seven wonders but their writings have not survived, except as references. The seven wonders included the:

- Great Pyramid of Giza
- Hanging Gardens of Babylon
- The Statue of Zeus at Olympia
- The Temple of Artemis at Ephesus
- The Mausoleum of Maussollos at Halicarnassus
- The Colossus of Rhodes
- The Lighthouse of Alexandria

In the 19th and early 20th centuries, some writers claimed that lists of wonders of the world have existed during the Middle Ages, although it is unlikely that these lists originated at that time because the word medieval was not invented until the Enlightenment-era, and the concept of a Middle Age did not become popular until the 16th century. Brewer's refers to them as "later list[s]" suggesting the lists were created after the Middle Ages.

Many of the structures on these lists were built much earlier than the Medieval Ages, but were well known. These lists go by names such as Wonders of the Middle Ages (implying no specific limitation to seven), Seven Wonders of the Middle Ages, Medieval Mind and Architectural Wonders of the Middle Ages.

Typically representative are:

- Stonehenge
- The Coliseum
- The Catacombs of Kom el Shoqafa
- The Great Wall of China
- The Porcelain Tower of Nanjing
- The Hagia Sophia
- The Leaning Tower of Pisa

Other sites sometimes included on such lists:

- Taj Mahal
- Cairo Citadel
- Ely Cathedral
- Cluny Abbey

Look at any of these works and you see the results of project management.

Until 1900 civil engineering projects were generally managed by creative architects, engineers, and master builders themselves, among those for example Vitruvius (1st century BC), Christopher Wren (1632–1723), Thomas Telford (1757–1834) and Isambard Kingdom Brunel (1806–1859). It was in the 1950s that organizations started to systematically apply project management tools and techniques to complex engineering projects.

As a discipline, Project Management developed from several fields of application including civil construction engineering, and heavy defense activity.[Two forefathers of project management are Henry Gantt, called the father of planning and control techniques, who is famous for his use of the Gantt chart as a project management tool; and Henri Fayol or his creation of the 5 management functions which form the foundation of the body of knowledge associated with project and program management. Both Gantt and Fayol were students of Frederick Winslow Taylor's theories of scientific management. His work is the forerunner to modern project management tools including work breakdown structure (WBS) and resource allocation. The 1950s marked the beginning of the modern Project Management era where core engineering fields come together working as one. Project management became recognized as a distinct discipline arising from the management discipline with engineering model. In the United States, prior to the 1950s, projects were managed on an *ad hoc* basis using mostly Gantt Charts, and informal techniques and tools. At that time, two mathematical project-scheduling models were developed. The "Critical Path Method" (CPM) was developed as a joint venture between DuPont Corporation and Remington Rand Corporation for managing plant maintenance projects. And the "Program Evaluation and Review Technique" or PERT, was developed by Booz Allen Hamilton as part of the United States Navy's (in conjunction with the Lockheed Corporation) Polaris missile submarine program. These mathematical techniques quickly spread into many private enterprises.

At the same time, as project-scheduling models were being developed, technology for project cost estimating, cost management, and engineering economics was evolving, with pioneering work by Hans Lang and others. In 1956, the American Association of Cost Engineers (now AACE International the Association for the Advancement of Cost Engineering) was formed by early practitioners of project management and the associated specialties of planning and scheduling, cost estimating, and cost/schedule control (project control). AACE continued its pioneering work and in 2006 released the first integrated process for portfolio, program and project management (Total Cost Management Framework).

The International Project Management Association (IPMA) was founded in Europe in 1967, as a federation of several national project management associations. IPMA maintains its federal structure today and now includes member associations on every continent except Antarctica. IPMA offers a Four Level Certification program based on the IPMA Competence Baseline (ICB). The ICB covers technical competences, contextual competences, and behavioral competences.

In 1969, the Project Management Institute (PMI) was formed in the USA. PMI publishes A Guide to the Project Management Body of Knowledge (PMBOK Guide), which describes project management practices that are common to "most projects, most of the time." PMI also offers multiple certifications.

Project Management Fundamentals

Foundations of Project Management

A project is defined as a temporary endeavor designed to provide a specific program, product or service to a specific client or group. Projects differ from programs in that a program is an ongoing series of activities associated with a specific client or group.

Project management can be quite complex. There are often any number of variables, risks, and stakeholders to deal with. In addition, projects require people to accomplish the needed tasks. Last, projects represent change; a move from the current state of doing things to some future desired or required state. Change naturally brings uncertainty and uncertainty itself carries a measure of risk. Given the reality that all of these different pieces operate in the same space it only make sense to work within a standardized approach. Doing this greatly increases the likelihood the project will be successful and the goal will be accomplished.

This material focuses on the project management methodology endorsed by the Project Management Institute (PMI).

What is Project Management?

Before we begin to dive into the specific of project management from a PMI perspective let's take a quick look at management in general. From this perspective management is defined as accomplishing needed tasks in a timely and efficient manner to the required level of quality.

The established and agreed upon functions of management include:

1. **Planning** in organizations and public policy is both the organizational process of creating and maintaining a plan; and the psychological process of thinking about the activities required to create a desired goal on some scale. As such, it is a fundamental property of intelligent behavior. This thought process is essential to the creation and refinement of a plan, or integration of it with other plans, that is, it combines forecasting of developments with the preparation of scenarios of how to react to them. An important, albeit often ignored aspect of planning, is the relationship it holds with forecasting. Forecasting can be described as predicting what the future will look like, whereas planning predicts what the future should look like.

2. **Organizing** is the act of rearranging elements following one or more rules. Anything is commonly considered organized when it looks like everything has a correct order or placement. But it's only ultimately organized if any element has no difference on time taken to find it. In that sense, organizing can also be defined as to place different objects in logical arrangement for better searching.

3. **Coordination** is the act of coordinating, making different people or things work together for a goal or effect.

4. **Directing** is associated providing in guidance to activities once they are in process, including specific instructions, feedback, advice, and recommendations with the intent of keeping things moving according to plan.

5. **Controlling** is an important function because it helps to check the errors and to take the corrective action so that deviation from standards are minimized and stated goals of the organization are achieved in desired manner. According to modern concepts, control is a foreseeing action whereas earlier concepts of control were used only when errors were detected. Control in management means setting standards, measuring actual performance and comparing it to expectations and taking corrective action when needed.

Project management is simply a more focused application of general management practices. PMI project management breaks the process down into 5 Process Groups comprised of 42 associated project management processes. The PMI Process Groups are:

1. Initiating

2. Planning

3. Executing

4. Monitoring and Controlling

5. Closing

From a PMI perspective managing a project generally addresses and includes:

1. Identifying requirements.

2. Addressing and understanding the various stakeholders needs, concerns and expectations as the project is planned and executed.

3. Managing overall project execution and client service delivery within the various project constraints:

    ○ Scope

    ○ Quality

    ○ Schedule

    ○ Budget

    ○ Resources

    ○ Risk

It is important to keep in mind that these constraints are interrelated to one and other. A change in one area is going to affect other project performance factors. For example, if there is a change in scope that causes the project to be expanded adjustments are going to have to be made in terms of time, cost, number of personnel assigned, resource requirements, etc.

Questions to Consider

1. How are the principles of management currently applied in your organization?

2. How is the effectiveness of the application of these principles measured?

3. What are the opportunities for improvement in this regard?

4. How are these opportunities being acted on?

5. What role does or will Project Management play in acting on these opportunities?

6. How are the Project Management processes being applied in this regard?

7. How is the effectiveness of the application of these Project Management methods, tools and processes being evaluated?

8. What are the opportunities for improvement in this regard?

Is it a Project? A Program? A Portfolio?

The answer to this question is important because these elements comprise a large portion of an organizations strategy. Let's start by briefly defining each.

As mentioned, a project is a temporary endeavor designed to produce a specific program, product or service. A program is one or more initiatives that are designed and undertaken to provide a long-term impact or outcome. A portfolio is comprised of one or more programs. Portfolios are created and sustained with the intent of providing a long-term competitive advantage to an organization or business. Let's look at an example.

Take a business that has decided to differentiate itself based on its ability to consistently deliver unique, cutting edge products to its customers. This organization would have a portfolio of business activities (programs) that could include research and development, manufacturing, and marketing. Each of these areas would manage their program-based activities to achieve maximum effectiveness and efficiency, both within their specific areas and across the other business areas. One method that would enable them to do this is to engage in specific projects that would enable

53

them to continuously improve their own operations and those of their partner operations or associated business units. Let's now look at each area in even greater detail, specifically in terms of scope, change, planning, management, success and monitoring.

Projects must have defined objectives. This enables the resources to be allocated in the way that leads to the required outcomes. Projects are also characterized by scope being progressively elaborated throughout the project lifecycle. What this means is as the project progresses the project delivery team (and even the client) will get additional insight and clarity into the specific deliverables that will best meet the targeted need. Progressive elaboration does not mean that things will be continuously added to what is expected from the project. This is known as "scope creep". Progressive elaboration is a natural part of the project life cycle. Scope creep on the other is not something that is beneficial to a project.

Change characterizes a project, specifically moving from a defined current state to a desired or required future state. Project personnel should also expect and plan for change to be part of the project execution and delivery project itself. Part of this is a function of the progressive elaboration mentioned earlier. It can also result from changes to project time-lines, resourcing, and client needs or expectations. Project managers plan for these types of changes and build appropriate change identification, tracking, and management processes into the overall project design.

Planning enables the project manager and project team to clarify what needs to be done, how it will be done, and the manner in which it needs to be done. The project process generally begins with an identified need and initial

54

thinking and planning as to methods that could be used to fulfill the requirements. As the project progresses both the needs and the methods by which to fulfill them will be clarified as well as continually aligned. As mentioned earlier, progressive elaboration is a natural element of the project management, execution and client service delivery process. Both awareness of and methods to effectively address must be integrated into the project management and execution mindset as well as the tools used in these processes.

Project success is measured in a variety of ways. The first and often most obvious methods is the by assessing the quality and timeliness of delivery. Cost of deliverables is also a major factor. Other factors that can be used to assess project success include customer and project team perspective on overall performance of the project team, the ability of future projects and project teams to leverage lessons learned from the current effort, and willingness of project team members to partner on future initiatives.

Because projects can span long periods of time, consume large amounts of resources, and be critical enablers for overall organizational success, their progress and performance must be measured and evaluated throughout the entire project lifecycle. In order to provide effective control the measurement processes must be an integral part of the project planning, overall execution, and client service delivery process.

Programs are comprised of one or more projects. For example, an organization seeking to improve its overall customer service and client service delivery system could engage in a Client Service Delivery Improvement Program. The program could include two projects. One of the projects could involve upgrading the customer service tracking and data management systems. The other could focus on improving customer service provider skills.

With this in mind it's obvious that programs have a larger scope and can be expected to require significantly more benefits than a single project event. A key element to keep in mind is to ensure all projects are aligned with specific business needs and client opportunities. Beginning with the overall strategic need and working backwards to determine what must be done to achieve these outcomes is a core element of strategic thinking, planning and execution.

Because programs are often comprised of one or more projects change can be very much the norm. Program managers must incorporate a strategic, programmatic perspective into their thinking in order to be able to anticipate and act on change. The program manager should also keep in mind that change will come from both inside the program and the projects associated with it, as well as from outside of the program (other areas and programs within the business for example). Methods and tools should be an integral part of the program management approach to enable personnel to identify, track, address and manage these changes effectively.

While separate and distinct projects can sometimes be rolled up into a single program, it is much more effective if the programmatic areas and opportunities are identified first. This allows specific opportunities to be identified within the programmatic area, the result being targeted project implementations that address the strategic needs and opportunities the organization has decided to pursue. When approached this way the program manager develops the overall program plan. This overall programmatic planning guides follow-on project planning.

Just as project managers oversee and are responsible for the overall execution and success for the event, program managers are responsible for the overall execution and success of the programmatic area. This includes ensuring activities and outcomes are consistently in alignment with strategic organizational needs, goals and opportunities. Perhaps more important, it also includes the need and opportunity to provide an overall vision and direction for the work being done. This enables team members to understand how the work they are doing connects to and supports the broader strategic agenda the organization is seeking to achieve. The role also encompasses the need for frequent communication, ensuring everyone who is involved with, impacted by or associated with the project has a clear understanding of what is going on.

As mentioned, programs encompass one or more projects and groups of activity with the overarching goal being to enhance the ability of the organization to service and support clients. The scope of assessing program success is much broader than that applied to projects. In addition the success factors projects are held accountable to (speed, cost and quality) programs are also responsible to ensure the overall set of initiatives provides the desired or required return on investment to the organization. Program managers should design and incorporate methods that will enable them to track project and program performance both in process and after project completion. Being able to track and measure interim success increases stakeholder confidence in the ability of the work effort to achieve the desired or required results.

The third level of focus is on the portfolio. Business portfolios encompass activities that align with and support the organizations strategic business objectives. As the business objectives change the focus on construct of the portfolio will change. This is important for the portfolio manager to constantly attend to. Failure to do so can cause the work the business is doing to quickly get out of alignment with what the business is working to or needs to achieve.

Change management is an integral part of business portfolio management. Change that can affect the portfolio can come from a number of different areas. They include changing client and customer needs and preferences, change in local, regional, national and international economic cycles, changes to local, regional, national or even international legislation and business practices, etc. Because the portfolio manager is responsible for activities that keep the organization in alignment with what is a very dynamic business environment they must leverage a variety of sources and systems to stay current on what is going on, both inside and outside the organization.

Planning puts the portfolio manager in a position to oversee and provide input to the myriad of different processes and projects the business will be involved in. This work is essential to helping it remain in alignment with customer opportunities and the changes that are constantly taking place in the business environment. Planning also helps to ensure limited resources are used and applied in the most effective and efficient manner.

Portfolio management involves planning, coordinating, controlling and evaluating the variety of activities associated with sustaining the operations and supporting business activities. When done properly it maximizes the activities going on within different functional and project execution arenas. This enables maximum impact and economies driven by scale to be achieved simultaneously.

Successful portfolio managers are those who are able to consistently deliver the kinds of large-scale impacts across multiple client bases and populations in a highly efficient manner. This ability leads to immediate return on investment and profitability. It also creates a stable, sustainable business model based on a clear, consistent applied set of business practices.

Monitoring at the portfolio level involves attending to many of the same business performance metrics that are commonly viewed by the general business community. These include profit and loss, stake price, return on assets, return on equity, etc. This type of monitoring also focuses on internal organizational metrics including project execution, use of resources, where funding for internal initiatives is secured from, staffing levels and needs, real-estate needs, acquisitions and divestitures, etc.

You can see how each level of management, specifically portfolio, program, and project, builds upon and from the others. Each level is highly reliant on and provides essential input to the other levels. This type of alignment if properly organized and executed can have powerful impact on overall business performance and client service delivery. The key is to understand what is being done, why it is being done, and how things are being done.

Questions to Consider

1. How does your organization currently leverage the organizational concept of Portfolio, Program and Project?

2. What types of projects is your organization currently involved in?

3. What types of projects are planned?

4. How do these current and planned projects fit into the organizations programmatic activities?

5. How do these programmatic activities fit into and align with the organizations overall portfolio management?

6. How do these activities align with and support the strategic objectives the organization is seeking to achieve?

7. How is the effectiveness of the individual and collective activities associated with the work associated with the projects, programs and overall portfolio evaluated?

8. What are the opportunities for improvement?

Why Project Management?

Projects span the range of complexity, from a simple set of activities covering a few days to multiple sets of complex interactions that span years or even decades. Project management brings stability and predictability to the activity by recommending they be planned, performed and evaluated in a structured, logical, thoughtful manner.

This is important for several reasons. First, projects are undertaken in the context of a larger set of circumstances. There are numerous stakeholders to address, legislative and environmental consideration, limited resources that others are competing for, etc. In addition, projects represent change. Change creates uncertainty. Uncertainty can create tension that if not addressed can lead to major problems across a variety of clients, stakeholders and groups.

Because project management provides a systematic approach to undertaking an event it provides for addressing the needs of those who will be involved and impacted. Successful projects also optimize the use of scarce resources and it reduces uncertainty by supporting the creation of a clear, visible path from the current state to the future desired or required state.

As we have discussed, projects are often planned and executed as a result of as well part of an overall strategic planning process and agenda. From a strategic perspective projects are typically authorized and undertaken as part of and in support of one or more of the following:

1. Market demand – Example – an auto company initiate a project to improve fuel economy in response increasing fuel prices and greater environmental awareness
2. Strategic opportunity – Example – an auto company initiates a project to begin building hybrid or all electric automobiles in response to greater availability of specialized battery technology.
3. Customer Request – Example – a homebuilder initiates a project to begin marketing services supporting installation of electrical automobile recharging stations in residential homes.
4. Technological Advance – Example – per the example of the high efficiency batteries discussed in the area of Strategic opportunity, such

opportunities are often a result of a technological advance.

5. Legal requirements – Example – a change in regulations governing financial disclosure to credit card customers creates the opportunity for a project to align marketing efforts with the disclosure effort and investment.

It is important to note that the strategic drivers mentioned above often work in concert with one and other. For example, although the Internet was created in the late 1960's as a means to enable scientist to communicate and share information with one and other, it did not really take off on a national or international scale until the mid 1990's. Why? Because a variety of other strategic activities and outcomes had to be in place. These include the growth in the PC market (which began in the early 1980's), development of methods (hardware and software) to connect PCs together on a very large scale, and demonstration to consumers that access and use of such systems could add personal value and fill needs they had.

Projects, be they within a program or part of a larger portfolio, are the means and methods by which organizations achieve specific goals and objectives. They are often most effective when this effort is part of the larger strategic agenda, planning and execution process. Although a single project or even group of projects can provide definitive benefits, they can also provide even more substantial returns when supporting the larger portfolios or programs the organization is involved in.

Questions to Consider

1. How are projects currently leveraged in your organization?
2. What factors are used to drive the creation, initiation, and execution of projects in your organization?
3. What types of initiatives are organized and acted upon as projects?
4. How are these projects aligned with overall organizational objectives?
5. How is the effectiveness of these activities evaluated?
6. What are the opportunities for improvement in this regard?
7. How would improvement in this area impact overall business performance and client service delivery?

Project Management Office

Although projects are temporary endeavors they can span several weeks, months or in some cases even years. In addition, they can encompass the efforts of dozens to hundreds or even thousands of people and the investment of huge sums of money. A Project Management Office (PMO) is established in some organizations to provide centralized and coordinated management for projects that fall within its areas of responsibility. As mentioned, a primary goal of portfolio management is to maximize the value of the investment associated with the myriad of programs and related projects. The PMO can play a central role in this process by ensuring opportunities to leverage work, resources and impact across projects and programs is maximized. The PMO can achieve these ends in a variety of ways, including:

1. Managing shared resources across all projects being administered by the PMO.
2. Coordinating communication across projects.
3. Identifying, developing and leveraging common project management methodology and tools as well as best practices and standards across all areas.
4. Researching, developing and maintaining project management policies, procedures, templates, and other shared project documentation.
5. Providing coaching, mentoring, and training support of project team members, clients, stakeholders, and other impacted groups.
6. Monitoring compliance with project management standards and performance criteria through regular performance reporting as well as project audits.

It is important to keep the responsibilities of the Project Manager and the PMO separate and distinct. While both ultimately focus on the needs of the organization, they pursue their focus and areas of responsibility differently. These differences include:

1. The Project Manager focuses on achieving the specific project objectives and requirements.
2. The PMO manages scope changes across projects that can position the organization to better achieve overarching strategic objectives.
3. The Project Manager aligns the assigned resources to achieve the best project outcomes.

4. The PMO optimizes the use of shared resources across all projects the organization is involved with and that fall under their scope of responsibility.
5. The Project Manager manages project execution and client service delivery within the triple constraints of speed, cost and quality.
6. The PMO has responsibility for managing the methods, standards, risk / reward, and inter-dependencies among projects.

Questions to Consider

1. How is the concept of the PMO applied in your organization?
2. How does this structure, or the absence of it, affect project risk management in your organization?
3. How is the effectiveness of the application of this organizational management and control structure evaluated?
4. What are the opportunities for improvement?
5. How would improvement in this area impact overall project and program execution?
6. How would improvement in this area impact overall business performance and client service delivery?

Project Management vs. Operations Management

Sometimes, when looking for someone to perform as a project manager there is the temptation to taking a strong operations manager in an area that is going to be affected by the project and assign them to the role of project manager. When the person does not do as well as expected or as needed those who assigned the person will standard back and wonder what happened. The reality is that both roles require different competencies. Failure to recognize this often contributes to problems with project execution.

Operations encompass functions and activities performed by the organization or business that provide the same product or a repetitive service, output, or deliverable. Examples of operations include check and transaction processing in the financial services industry, manufacturing operations in the auto, electronics or garment industry, and production of various types of food in the packaged goods industry. The important thing to keep in mind about operations management is the overarching goal of producing output of consistent quality, in the required quantities, within specific cost guidelines.

Project management involves a focus on a temporary set of activities that lead to a specific outcome. The work associated with projects is unique to the specific event based on the required outputs, the resources required and available to produce the output, and the amount of time available to complete the work associated with it.

While projects are often initiated to improve a specific set of or type of operation, the jobs of project manager and operations manager are distinctly different. The project manager is the person assigned by the responsible organization to achieve the identified project objectives.

Specific competencies associated with successful performance in the role of project manager include:

1. Knowledge – including deep, application level understanding of and experience with project

management techniques. Knowledge of the specific area and technology associated with the area the project will be impacting is useful as well.

2. Performance – the ability to execute effectively even when under high stress.
3. Decisive – the knowledge, ability and experience to make correct decisions even when lacking complete information.
4. Dealing with ambiguity – the skill to handle uncertainty in a manner that prevents it from unnecessarily delaying project execution and client service delivery.
5. Communication – the ability and willingness to provide the information needed by a variety of team members, clients and stakeholders when they need it and in the manner that is most effective for them. This competency also includes the ability to create and sustain a performance environment that fosters and depends on open, honest and timely communication among all team members, clients, and stakeholders.

Questions to Consider

1. How does your organization currently differentiate between project management and operations management?
2. What competencies have been identified and are associated with successful performance in an Operations Management role?
3. What competencies have been identified and are associated with successful performance in a Project Management role?

4. What are the similarities? What are the differences? How are these similarities and differences taken into account and addressed when staffing these types of positions?
5. How do the differences and / or similarities affect project risk management in your organization?
6. What are the opportunities for improvement in this regard?
7. How would improving in this area impact overall project execution, business performance and client service delivery?

The Environment Projects are Executed In

Projects, programs and portfolios are managed and executed within the organizations they support. They affect and are affected by the same factors that impact the enterprise as a whole, including:

1. The existing organizational culture and structure
2. The processes the organization currently uses to conduct its business
3. Government regulations
4. Industry standards
5. Product standards
6. Litigation
7. Infrastructure
8. Human capital
9. Market conditions
10. Competition
11. Political climate
12. Risk tolerances
13. Stakeholder demands
14. Organizational communication
15. Access to funding, resources and raw materials

Just like organizational leadership, project managers and associated project personnel must understand the factors comprising the environment they are operating in. Failure to do so can cause the project to miss the mark in terms of delivering on expected or required outputs and in the process damage the organizations ability to conduct business in the required manner.

Questions to Consider

1. What methods does your organization currently use to track and address the internal and external factors that drive, affect and influence organizational performance?
2. How are these methods affect project risk management activities?
3. How do these factors affect the selection of projects the organization chooses to engage in or elects not to engage in?
4. How is the effectiveness and impact of these methods evaluated?
5. What are the opportunities for improvement in this regard?
6. How would improvement in this area affect overall project execution?
7. How would improvement in this area affect overall business performance and client service delivery?

Project Life Cycle

Overview

As you can see through the previous discussion projects are collections of sequenced activities that when properly acted upon lead to a specific, needed outcome. The term life cycle is used to describe the process based on the idea that projects have a distinct beginning, middle, and end point.

The benefit to taking a life-cycle perspective to projects is that it enables a specific methodology to be developed and applied to the activities associated with the work. Through use and experience the methodology can be refined to the point that it can be applied consistently and effectively across a number of different project applications. The strength of a well-defined methodology is that it can be quickly and effectively learned by a large number of people but allows for enough flexibility to allow it to be adjusted to a variety of situations and circumstance. The project life cycle then becomes the framework for managing the work regardless of the specific work involved.

Characteristics of the Project Life Cycle

No matter what the size, scope of type of application projects are associated with they can all be mapped to the same basically life-cycle:

1. Start-up
2. Organizing
3. Preparing
4. Execution
5. Closure

During project start-up the overall cost is comparatively low. Costs will steadily increase during in support of the activities associated with organizing and preparing. They will reach their peak during activities supporting execution, the part of the project where the actual client deliverables are designed, created, built, tested, delivered and installed. This part of the life cycle generally involves the most personnel and resources and consumes most of the project schedule as well. Activities associated with project closure see costs drop off dramatically to conclusion.

Aside from the time and cost profiles associated with the different phases of the project life cycle, there are a few other important points to take note of.

1. Uncertainty is greatest at the beginning of a project.
2. The opportunity for stakeholders to influence project outcomes without significantly affecting cost or schedule is greatest at the beginning portion of the project life cycle.
3. The risk to stakeholders is greatest at the start of the project.
4. The cost and risk associated with changes to the project increases as the project progresses.
5. These risks drop as the project progresses because uncertainty is reduced.

Questions to Consider

1. How does your organization currently apply the philosophy and practice associated with a project management life cycle?

2. How does your organization position project risk management work in the context of the overall project management life cycle?
3. How does the application of the life-cycle approach to project management enhance project execution and client service delivery?
4. How is performance in this regard measured and tracked?
5. What are the opportunities for improvement?
6. How would improvement in this area enhance overall project execution and client service delivery?

The Relationship Between Project and Product Life cycles

As mentioned, the project life cycle consists of:

1. Start-up
2. Organizing
3. Preparing
4. Execution
5. Closure

Compare this with the product life cycle that consists of:

1. Introduction – consisting of positioning against competitors, branding to introduce of differentiate, pricing for position, promotion and distribution.
2. Growth – consisting of production in required quantities and to required levels of quality, pricing to remain competitive against new and

existing entrants, promotion to larger, more diverse audiences, and efficient distribution to those markets and customers.
3. Maturity – consisting of continuing to enhance the product in an efficient, high quality manner, uses of incentives and logistics to enhance and sustain effective distribution, and promotion focusing on continuous differentiation.
4. Decline – consisting of options including continuing to differentiate to maintain market share, harvest remaining profits by using ideas in new areas or selling the product to another group, or discontinuing the line and investing the resources into new development to start the process over again.

The relationship between projects and products can be dynamic. Projects can be initiated to create a new product, introduce new products to the market, or focus on changes to facilitate their growth. Projects can be initiated to rebrand an existing product, to enhance features. Projects can be initiated to reconfigure production, manufacturing or logistics to improve the efficiency or effectiveness of those processes.

While projects can be introduced to improve the efficiency and effectiveness of operations, projects themselves also need to be executed in an efficient manner as well. Breaking a project down into Phases can help in this area.

Questions to Consider

1. How are projects in your organization aligned with the product life cycle?

2. How does this alignment support your organizations overall business strategy?
3. How is the effectiveness of this alignment tracked and measured?
4. What are the opportunities for improvement in the area of alignment of projects to the organizational product cycle?
5. What is needed for the organization to capitalize on these opportunities?
6. How would improving in this area impact overall organizational effectiveness?

Project Phases

Projects are broken down into phases to provide project personnel with the control needed to execute effectively and support excellent overall client service delivery. As mentioned, the project life cycle can be broken down into specific components, consisting of:

1. Start-up
2. Organizing
3. Preparing
4. Execution
5. Closure

These five elements can be further defined as project phases, specifically:

1. Initiation
2. Planning
3. Execution
4. Monitor and control
5. Close

These project phases are typically performed in a sequential manner. The phase approach allows the project to be broken down or divided into logical subsets of activities and resource allocation. This provides project personnel with a better measure of control over the activities occurring within the particular phase. The need for phases, the number of phases and the degree of control depend on the size, complexity, scope, risk and potential risk associated with the project. Regardless of the number of phases a project encompasses, all of the phases associated with it share similar characteristics, including:

1. When phases are sequential the close of a specific phase involves a transfer or some form of hand-off of the work to personnel involved in the next phase. This end phase point represents a logical point to pause and evaluate the effort and results to that point to determine next steps and even the viability of continuing with the project. These end points are commonly referred to as decision gates, kill points, milestones, phase exits, phase gates, or stage gates.

2. The work performed in each phase has a distinct focus, specific to the needs of that phase. For example, the needs and work associated with Start-up are unique to that phase. This is important because the specific needs determine the type of resourcing and personnel competencies needed to successfully perform the work associated with the phase.

3. An extra degree of control is needed to enable the primary objective of a specific phase to be achieved. The fact that processes are repeated across the process groups provides this level of control as well as defining the boundaries of each stage.

It is important to keep in mind that there is no one best way to define or manage a project. It is true that practices within an industry will often lead to a defined, standardized and generally accepted set of procedures. It is equally quite common to see a significant amount of variation in terms of practices, processes and procedures across firms within the same industry. For example, one firm may see a feasibility study as a fundamental element of Initiation while another firm in the same industry may see the same type of study as a part of planning. (My personal perspective is the feasibility study is a part of the process associated with pre-initiation or initiation. The project has to be feasible, that is having a good likelihood of success, before committing resources to it).

There are a couple of additional elements associated with the project life-cycle we need to understand with regard to the importance of project phases, specifically project governance across the life-cycle and the relationships between and across the project phases.

Questions to Consider

1. How is the phased approach to project management applied to project execution in your organization?

2. What is the relationship between the phased approach to project management and project risk management in your organization?
3. How is the effectiveness of the application of the phased approach to project management and execution evaluated?
4. What are the opportunities for improvement in this regard?
5. How would improvement in this area effect project execution and overall client service delivery?

Governance Across the Project Life cycle

Projects are temporary endeavors designed to provide a specific output. They often create some type of move from a current state of operations or way of thinking about things to some new state. As such they represent change. Because change creates uncertainty it is important for organizations to have some type of oversight to ensure the processes, methods and approaches being used to help create and drive the change are being properly applied and are delivering the correct results. This is where governance comes into play.

Governance provides comprehensive and consistent oversight to project activities. This oversight creates a much greater likelihood of the project being completed successfully because it allows both risks and opportunities to be identified and managed as early and as effectively as possible.

The approach and methods to project governance should be described in the project management plan. Why? Because project governance fits within the larger scope of the overall plan and the project management plan is where this information is profiled.

Projects are executed within the triple constrains of time, cost and quality. Phases allow the work to be segmented in such a way that logical groupings of tasks and activities can be resourced and performed most effectively. Monitoring, measuring and reporting project performance within and across each of the phases and in the context of the triple constraints are what project governance is all about.

Questions to Consider

1. How is project governance applied to projects your organization engages in?
2. How does project governance add value to the project management, project execution, and client service delivery your organization supports?
3. What is the relationship between project governance and project risk management in your organization?
4. How is the effectiveness of the approaches taken and tools and methods used for project governance evaluated?
5. What are the opportunities for improvement in the area of project governance?
6. How would improvement in this area effect overall project execution and client service delivery?

Relationships Between and Across Project Phases

A project phase represents a period of time during which specific project tasks and activities are accomplished. While the on paper the phases appear separate and distinct it is important to keep in mind that the work of each project phase will feed into the one that follows it. For example, each project phase will have specific deliverables associated with it and that come from it. These deliverables will often provide the foundation for the phase that follows.

In terms of relationships among phases there are three basic ones to keep in mind. The first is a sequential relationship. This type of relationship is present when one phase needs to be complete before the project can proceed into the next. This type of relationship reduces uncertainty but may also eliminate options for reducing the schedule. The second type of relationship involves overlapping phases, when the next phase starts before the current stage is completed. While this type of overlap can shorten the overall project schedule it can also increase the amount of risk if subsequent phases have to work with less than complete information. The third type of relationship among project phases is known as iterative. This type of relationship is characterized by only one phase of work being planned at a time. This allows for planning of subsequent phases to be planned based on more complete information from the phase that comes before it. While this can reduce uncertainty and associated risk it can also increase the time required to complete the project as well as costs.

Deciding how to organize and execute a project in this regard is based on what is known or not known about the project, the current and projected future state of required technology, availability of and access to resources, risk, etc.

Questions to Consider

1. What are the relationships that exist between and exist across project phases that your organization is involved in?
2. How are these relationships managed?
3. How are the risks associated with these relationships identified and managed?
4. How is the management of these relationships evaluated?
5. What are the opportunities for improvement in this area?
6. How would improvement in this area effect overall project management, execution and client service delivery?

The Work of Projects and the Work of Organizations

Project work and the work of organizations share several common characteristics including:

1. The work is performed by people, both as teams and as individuals
2. The ability to perform the work and deliver the required outputs is limited by the impact of the triple constraints – time, money, and level of quality required.
3. The work is planned, executed, managed, monitored and controlled.
4. The work is performed in support of and to enable the organization to achieve larger organizational goals and objectives.

83

Projects also have a direct impact on organizational work, specifically:

1. Projects are temporary endeavors, initiated to provide a specific output in support of a specific goal or objective by a specific date in a specific configuration.
2. Organizational work is characterized by repetitive work that focuses on providing a specific output for a specific purpose in a specific manner by a specific time.
3. Projects are often created to enable the organization to either perform more effectively in their current state or to enable it to provide a new service.
4. Organizational work and project work often compete for the same resources.
5. Leaders of the organization and of projects within the organization must work effectively together if the goals of both are going to be achieved in the most efficient, effective manner possible.

Questions to Consider

1. How are the relationships between temporary work generally associated with projects and the longer-term day-to-day work associated with on-going operations integrated and managed in your business?
2. How is the effectiveness of this work evaluated?
3. What is the impact of the interrelatedness of these sets of activities on overall business performance?
4. What are the opportunities for improvement?
5. How would improvement in this area affect overall business performance?

Stakeholders

Stakeholders are people or organizations that are actively involved, interested or impacted by the work the project is doing of the output the project will produce. Because stakeholders can exert influence over project performance and outcomes it is important to know who they are, their interests, fears, hopes, and aspirations, and how they can impact of influence the work the project is doing. Once stakeholders have been identified the project teams is in a better position to understand their specific needs and to manage their reactions and responses to their needs in the most effective, appropriate manner possible.

Common categories of stakeholders include:

1. Customers and users – the individuals or organizations that will use the products are services the project produces. Customers and users may be internal to the organization or external. There may also be multiple layers of customers for a specific products or service (automobiles for example – the dealers that sell them, the people who buy them, the parts stores that service them, the fuel stations that fill them, the firms that insure them).

2. Sponsor – this is the person or group that provides the financial and material resources and support that enables the project to move forward. From the outset the project sponsor champions the initiative. To achieve this end the sponsor serves as a spokesperson, promoting the benefits of the project to higher levels of organizational

management to gain and sustain support. The sponsor leads the event through the beginning phases up to and through initial authorization. They also play a major role in the development of the initial project scope and project charter. The sponsor also plays an important role in the issue escalation process. For issue and matters that cannot be resolved at the level of the project manager the sponsor provide a communication conduit to the top level of organizational leadership.

3. Portfolio management / portfolio review board – Portfolio management is responsible for high-level governance of a collection of projects that comprise a specific portfolio. These projects may or may not be interdependent. Portfolio review boards are comprised of senior organizational executives. They are responsible for determining which projects the organization will engage in based on the strategic needs and direction of the enterprise. They are also responsible for organizing projects into portfolios. Criteria for which projects to be included into a specific portfolio or organized into their own portfolio include cost, scope, focus, risk, etc.

4. Program manager – personnel assigned to this role are responsible for managing related projects in a manner that allows them to be collectively executed in the most effective and efficient manner possible while keeping risk within manageable or predicted levels. Program managers work with the various project managers

to ensure proper coordination and integration of effort.

5. Project management office – The PMO is an organizational entity that provides centralized and coordinated management of the projects that are assigned to its area of responsibility. The scope of PMO responsibilities can include providing project management support functions to actually being responsible for direct management of a project. The PMO can also be a stakeholder if it has either direct or indirect responsibility for the outcome of the project. Examples of support the PMO can provide include administrative support in the areas of policies, methods, tools and templates, support for project managers including training, coaching, and mentoring, resourcing, and communication among project managers, sponsors, managers and other stakeholders.

6. Project managers – personnel are assigned to these roles are responsible for ensuring the project provides expected deliverables in the manner planned and resourced for. A skilled project manager must have a solid understanding of the details of what needs to be done, but from a total systems perspective. Success in the project manager role requires flexibility, leadership, good judgment, communication skills, negotiation skills, and strong understanding and experience with project management methods and practices. The project manager is responsible for continuous communications with all stakeholders. They are

the central link between stakeholders and the project.

7. Project team – a project team consists of the project manager, project management team, and personnel who are responsible for carrying out the tasks required to deliver the project successfully. A successful project team is characterized by a diverse set of talents and experiences linked by the common goal of bringing the project in successfully.

8. Functional managers – functional managers are personnel who serve in function or activity specific roles that support overall project execution and performance. Functional managerial roles include areas such as HR, Training, Finance, Procurement, Technology, Operations, etc. It is also important to keep in mind that people serving in these functional roles may well be pulling double duty, specifically performing project work while maintaining their day-to-day functional responsibilities as well.

9. Operations management – personnel in operations management roles exercise responsibilities in core areas of the business, for example research, development, manufacturing, service, etc. Like functional managers, operations managers who are performing project work can also still be responsible for their day-to-day operational activities as well. They can also be clients in the project as well, specifically being recipients of the project deliverables.

10. Sellers and business partners – personnel and parties serving in these roles are those vendors, suppliers, contractors or other external groups that supply some type of program, product, service or support that is needed for successful execution of the project. Business partners are also external to the organization. However, their relationship with the business is based on some sort of front-end screening, certification or approval by organizational leadership. Business partners provide specialized expertise or provide a specialized service.

It is also important to realize that all stakeholders are not created equally. Towards that end it can be useful to differentiate stakeholders based on their involvement with the project and their importance to overall project performance and client service delivery. For example:

1. Which stakeholders are required for project success and whose needs and interests will be positively impacted by project performance and delivery?
2. Which stakeholders are required for project success and whose needs and interests will be negative impacted by project performance and delivery?
3. Which stakeholders are not required for project success and whose interests will be positively impacted by project performance and delivery?
4. Which stakeholders are not required for project success and whose interests will be negatively impacted by project performance and delivery?

As you look at this list of different stakeholder impact, needs and interests consider the following:

1. What are the different needs of the various stakeholder groups?
2. How should these needs be addressed?
3. Which group will potentially have the greatest impact on the likelihood of project success?
4. How would the needs of this group need to be managed to increase the likelihood of success?
5. What do you need to know about this specific group?
6. What do you need to know about all of the stakeholder groups?
7. How would you go about obtaining this information?

In addition to the myriad of stakeholders there are other factors that exert influence on project execution and management and the client service delivery that it is designed and intended to provide. The following discussion profiles this area.

Questions to Consider

1. How are project, program and portfolio stakeholders differentiated in your organization?
2. How are stakeholder risks identified, addressed and tracked at the various levels of project, program and portfolio management?
3. How is the impact of this differentiation evaluated?
4. What is the impact of this differentiation on project execution, project performance, program

and portfolio management and overall client service delivery?

5. What are the opportunities for improvement?
6. How would improvement in this area impact project management? Program management? Portfolio management? Overall client service delivery?

Organizational Culture

Culture is defined as the set of beliefs, norms, expectations and behaviors that define and guide the behavior of the organization and the people that comprise it. In order for a person to become a fully accepted member of an organization they must show the other members that they understand and abide by the norms and expectations that comprise and define the unit. An organizations unique culture can be identified using a number of everyday organizational behavioral and performance indicators including:

1. Vision
2. Values
3. Norms
4. Beliefs
5. Expectations
6. Policies
7. Methods
8. Procedures
9. View and perspective on authority
10. Employee engagement
11. Ethical behavior

Because culture defines the beliefs and behaviors of members of the organization it has a powerful impact on

91

employee and organizational performance. Because projects are a part of how organizations conduct their business, culture will have a strong impact in this area as well.

The culture of the organization is an environmental factor that influences the entire enterprise. To increase the likelihood of effectiveness project managers must understand the culture of the organization their projects are being executed in and in support of. For example, as we discussed earlier, projects represent change from some current state to some desired or required future state. Consider how such a project would be viewed in an organization that has a culture that has demonstrated the willingness and ability to embrace change vs. one that has not been successful with change in the past. Think about how the project manager would have to approach the clients, stakeholders and people being impacted by the project in each instance. Consider how the approaches would differ in order to increase the likelihood of support and success.

Another element of culture project managers needs to understand focuses on the aspect of projects being executed in a global environment. In cases like project manager and team members need to understand both the culture of the organization and the culture of the community the organization operates within. It is a mistake for project managers and team members to assume that all people operate and think the same way they do. Savvy project managers and team members invest the time and resources needed to understand the environment they are working in and the people they are working with.

Questions to Consider

1. How does your organization address culture and the impact it can have on project execution and client service delivery?
2. What does your organization do to ensure organizational culture is as closely aligned with business and operational needs as well as the needs of the market place and business environment?
3. How does organizational culture affect how project risk is addressed in your organization?
4. How effective is the current alignment?
5. How effective are the current risk management processes, procedures and tools?
6. What are the opportunities for improvement?
7. How would improvement in this area effect business performance and overall client service delivery?

Organizational Structure

Organizational structure defines the areas and scope of responsibility, hierarchy and reporting relationships among members of the group. Organizational structure is another environmental enterprise factor that can have an impact on project execution.

For most the organizational chart is the starting point in understanding how a business area is organized. However it is also important for project managers and team members to understand relationships and structures that are not reflected on the org chart. Organizational culture influences the perspective on how the relationships shown on the organizational chart are applied in the actual work environment. For example, in some organizations the org chart is adhered to very strictly. Members see it as a chain of command. Issues are escalated in a very systematic way, following the lines of communication and responsibility as they are defined on the organizational chart. They would never think of "jumping a level". Other organizations have a more fluid and dynamic approach to communication, reflected by the idea that people call and talk to who they need to talk to, regardless of where one or the other falls in the organizational hierarchy. The reality is that most organizations fall somewhere in between these two extremes. Members of the organization are able to exercise flexibility in terms of who they communicate with to a certain point, say two levels above them or two levels below them. Beyond that the organizational culture specifies they communicate through the various layers.

This discussion leads us to the idea that there are basically three types of organizational structures or designs applied in business. They are the functional, matrix and project.

Projects organized and executed around a functional organizational structure draw managers from the organizations various functional activities. Team members are grouped and organized based on functional specialties such as production, marketing, engineering, accounting, etc. Team members assigned to do project work based on their functional specialties often continue to maintain their functional responsibilities as well. This type of arrangement carries unique requirements for the project manager including:

94

1. Little or no authority or control over the functional managers and personnel working the project
2. Little or no control over resource availability
3. Little or no control over the project budget (the functional manager maintains control over resources and funding)
4. Being a member of a functional team themselves, the program manager role is part-time, performed in addition to their functional responsibilities
5. Because personnel providing administrative support to the project also come from functional areas within the organization they also serve the project in a part-time capacity

The second type of project organizational structure, the matrix, is a blend of characteristics representative of both the functional and projectized structures. This mix or blend of characteristics creates continuum of matrix types.

1. Weak matrix - The project manager has limited authority over project execution. The functional manager retains the majority of authority and the matrix manager is accountable to them. Projects executed in a weak matrix environment have limited access to resources as they remain under the authority, direction and control of the functional managers. The project manager role in a weak matrix environment is part-time, with the person continuing in their functional role as well. Administrative and support staff is part-time as well, with personnel performing in these roles still being responsible for their functional work as well.

2. Balanced matrix – The project manager's authority in this type of set-up is low to moderate, being based on the amount of autonomy the manager is provided. Resourcing falls into the same category. Project budgeting and resourcing is negotiated in this type of project set-up. The role of the project manager continues to be part-time, as they also maintain their functional responsibilities. Project support is also part-time as the personnel assigned to these roles continue to maintain their functional responsibilities.

3. Strong matrix – The project manager's authority in a strong matrix ranges from moderate to strong based on the amount of time and autonomy the project manager is given to work on project issues. Access to resources mirrors authority, specifically the greater the authority the greater the access to resources needed for successful execution. The strong matrix positions the project manager to control the project budget. The role of project manager is full time in this type of structure. Once the project is complete the project manager will move back to their functional role or some other assignment. Administrative support is also full-time in a strong matrix arrangement.

The third type of project organizational structure is the projectized. This type of structure sets the project team apart from other organizational activities by making it a functional organizational entity in and of itself. The project manager role is full-time. The person in the role has total control and authority for project execution and client service delivery in this type of set-up. As an autonomous organizational activity a projectized team also has access to and control over resources, personnel, funding and support.

Factors that can influence the type of organizational structure that is ultimately selected include:

1. Organizational culture
2. Access to talent
3. On-going production business requirements
4. Type of project
5. Scope of project
6. Risk associated with project

Questions to Consider

1. What type(s) or organizational structures does your business activity use in support of projects the organization is involved in?
2. How does the organizational structure affect project risk management in your organization?
3. How is the specific type of organizational structure selected?
4. How is it supported in terms of personnel resources, and funding?
5. How is the effectiveness of it in relation to project execution and client service delivery evaluated?
6. What are the opportunities for improvement?
7. How would improvement in this area affect project execution and client service delivery?

Organizational Process Assets

Organizational process assets include anything needed to influence or support successful project execution and client service delivery. Process assets include plans, policies, procedures, guidelines, tools, and templates. Also included are lessons learned, knowledge databases, and historical information. Risk information is also included in this category. Specifically, organizational process assets can be grouped into processes and procedures and corporate knowledge base.

Process and procedures assets include:

1. Standard operating procedures
2. Standard project and product life cycles
3. Quality policies and procedures
4. Standardized work instructions
5. Performance measurement criteria
6. Organizational communication requirements
7. Guidelines and requirements associated with project closure
8. Financial control procedures
9. Time management procedures
10. Issue and defect management procedures
11. Change control procedures
12. Risk control procedures
13. Work prioritization, approval, and issuing procedures

Corporate knowledge base assets include:

1. Databases supporting process measurement and reporting
2. Files associated with project management including scope, cost, schedule, and performance measurement baselines
3. Historical information
4. Lessons learned

5. Issue and defect management databases
6. Databases supporting configuration management
7. Financial and performance tracking databases including labor hours, cost, baseline, and variance.

Questions to Consider

1. What specific organizational process assets does your organization currently possess?
2. How are these assets identified in relation to the project work they support?
3. How are these assets leveraged in support of projects?
4. How do these assets enhance overall project performance and client service delivery?
5. How is the effectiveness of the use of these assets evaluated?
6. What are the opportunities for improvement in this regard?
7. How would improvement in this area affect project execution and client service delivery?

Project Management Processes

Overview

Effective project management involves the application of specific knowledge, skills, tools, methods, and techniques in the performance of specific project activities. The top end goal of this work is to achieve specific project goals and objectives.

As we peel back the process of project management it is clear that the processes associated with and in support of project execution and client service delivery are nothing more than a set of interrelated actions and activities that when performed together in the proper manner lead to a specific outcome. While all of this may seem quite obvious and quite simple, the reality is that it is all too easy to either confuse specific activities or perform them incorrectly. The results of even small performance errors can have a large impact on the projects overall ability to deliver.

In the process of project execution it is important for the project manager and team members to not only understand the processes and associated activities they are performing. They must also understand the context in which they are being performed, specifically constraints, environmental factors, resource limitations and anything else that could preclude or prevent success.

In order for the project to deliver required results the project team must:

1. Understand project requirements
2. Understand the environment in which the project will be executed
3. Understand which project tools and processes are available to them

4. Select the processes and tools that will generate the highest degree of project success
5. Apply a defined, well understood approach to overall project execution and client service delivery
6. Execute and deliver on the project within the requirements of stakeholder needs and expectations
7. Balance the multiple, simultaneously competing demands of scope, time, cost, quality, resources and risk in the process of deliver the required project outcomes

Questions to Consider

1. How does your organization currently work to understand project requirements?
2. How does your organization currently work to understand the environments the projects it is working on are being executed within?
3. Which tools and processes are made available to project personnel to enable them to perform project work to maximum effect?
4. What type of methodology does your organization apply to project management and execution as well as overall client service delivery?
5. How does your organization create and maintain stability, predictability and certainty from the clients' perspective that the project will deliver on identified commitments?
6. How does your organization leverage understanding project requirements to enable and enhance project risk management?

7. How is the current state of project performance and client service delivery measured?
8. What are the opportunities for improvement in the referenced areas?
9. How would improvement in these areas affect project execution and overall client service delivery?

Why apply project management processes?

1. Application of such processes ensures a structured, systematic approach.
2. Such an application reduces uncertainty by enabling people with the knowledge they need to perform specific project tasks and activities

There are generally two categories of project processes:

1. Project management processes focus on the effective flow of the project throughout its duration. Project management processes encompass the tools and techniques involved in the application of skills addressed in the specific Project Management Knowledge Areas.
2. Processes focusing on products provide the information and resources needed to create the project's product outcomes. Product oriented processes are normally defined by the project life-cycle. The scope of the project cannot be defined without some basic understanding of how to create the specified product.

The power of the project management processes comes from the fact that they are understood and applied on a large scale. This means that a person can move from project to project, region to region, industry to industry and still be able to perform effectively in the project environment. However, this does not mean that all project processes should be applied in the same way across all projects. Project managers and team members must take the time to learn and understand the specific requirements of each project they are working on and the environment it is being conducted in. This enables the project team to determine which project processes are most appropriate for the specific application and then to apply them with the required degree of discipline.

Project management is both an iterative and integrative process. It is iterative based on the notion that each successive step in project execution provides additional clarity. Each step in project execution also makes changes to the project or final project outcome more difficult. It is integrative because each step and process associated with project execution provides input into the steps and processes that follow it. This "building block" approach requires that execution and performance associated with and in support of each succeeding step be of the highest quality possible because of the potential or actual impact it can have on activities that follow it.

Because projects are temporary endeavors designed to produce a specific outcome they operate as a closed system within the organization. While they require input of data and resources from both within and often outside the organization the ultimate goal is to deliver some defined value back to the organization. The closed nature of projects, a system within a system, allows for and supports the specific project processes to be grouped into five categories. These are known as Project Management Process Groups. Keep in mind the Project Management Process Groups are not project phases. They are the logical grouping of project management processes. The Project Management Groups and associated processes are leveraged to complete work associated with each project phase. The groups are:

1. Initiation Process Group – defined by the processes performed to define a new project or a new phase of an existing project by obtaining the authorization needed to start the project or phase.
2. Planning Process Group – characterized by the processes required to establish project scope, refine project performance objectives, and define the type and course of action required to achieve the overall project and client service delivery objectives.
3. Executing Process Group – consists of the processes required to complete the work defined in the project management plan that will support the attainment of the project specifications and objectives.
4. Monitoring and Controlling Process Group – characterized by the processes used to track, review, and regulate the progress and performance of the project, determine which areas require change, and initiate the required change.
5. Closing Process Group – defined by the processes used to finalize all activities across all process groups to formally close the entire project or a specific phase within a project.

Questions to Consider

1. How can your organization improve its current project management methods?
2. How would improvement in this area impact overall client service delivery?
3. How would the use of Project Management Process Groups enhance project management and client service delivery in your organization?
4. What elements of this approach to project management and execution could be used to enhance project performance in your organization?

How Project Management Processes Interact

Project management processes are specific elements or sets of activities that are performed within the context of the greater whole of the project plan. While each process can be studied in its own right, in practice they overlap with one and other. The key to using the processes effectively and efficiently is to have a deep enough understanding of them both individually and collectively so that they are able to be leveraged, actioned, and evaluated to ensure maximum contribution to the success of the project. It is also important to keep in mind that project management processes are both iterative and repetitive. Specifically, each process will use the ones performed previous to it and build upon it and the same processes will be repeated throughout the project life-cycle.

Questions to Consider

1. What type of consideration does your organization currently give to the idea that project management processes interact with one and other as well as the broader organization?
2. How is the impact of the interactions measured?
3. What is the impact of the interactions on overall project performance and client service delivery?
4. How does this interactions affect project risk management?
5. What is the impact of these interactions on the larger organization?
6. What are the opportunities for improvement from a project execution perspective?
7. What are the opportunities for improvement from an organizational interaction perspective?
8. How would improvement in these areas impact overall project execution, client service delivery, and organizational performance as a whole?

PMI Project Management Process Groups

As mentioned, within the PMI project management framework there are five Process Groups. As mentioned previously, Project Management Process Groups and their associated processes are not Project Phases. The groups and processes represent the work that is done to accomplish what is required by each phase. Why the differentiation? First, several of the processes will be repeated throughout the execution of the project. Second, Project Phases represent the method by which a project will be organized and executed. The Process Groups and associated processes represent the means by which the work required in each of

109

the phases will be accomplished. The reality is that the work required in a particular phase can be approached in any number of different ways. For example, take a project that consists of the following phases:

1. Feasibility study
2. Concept development
3. Design
4. Prototype
5. Test
6. Build
7. Test
8. etc.

In a project like this, the Process Groups and associated processes would be leveraged and repeated across several of the project phase. The PMI approach being discussed here represents a recognized, accepted, disciplined approach to achieve the required outcomes. Since the Project Process Management Groups are independent of specific project phases or methodology they can be easily and effectively applied across different project types and different industries.

Questions to Consider

1. How are projects your organization is currently involved in or associated with organized and executed in terms of phases?
2. How are these phases currently identified?
3. How are these phases currently organized and sequenced?
4. How is the effectiveness of this methodology evaluated?

5. What role does this work play in the context of project risk management in your organization?
6. What are the opportunities for improvement?
7. How would improvement in this area impact project management and execution as well as overall client service delivery?

Within the five Process Groups there are 42 project management processes. The following represents the alignment of project management processes and the Process Groups.

1. Initiating Process Group
   - Develop Project Charter Processing
   - Identify Stakeholders Process

2. Planning Process Group
   - Develop Project Management Plan Process
   - Collect Requirement Process
   - Define Scope Process
   - Create Work Break Down Structure Process
   - Define Activities Process
   - Sequence Activities Process
   - Estimate Activities Resources Process
   - Estimate Activities Duration Process
   - Develop Schedule Process
   - Estimate Costs Process
   - Determine Budget Process
   - Plan Quality Process
   - Develop Human Resource Plan Process
   - Plan Communication Process
   - Plan Risk Management Plan Process
   - Identify Risks Process

- Perform Qualitative Risk Analysis Process
- Plan Risk Responses Process

3. Executing Process Group
   - Direct and Manage Project Execution Process
   - Perform Quality Assurance Process
   - Acquire Project Team Process
   - Develop Project Team Process
   - Manage Project Team Process
   - Information Distribution Process
   - Stakeholder Expectation Management Process
   - Procurement Process

4. Monitoring and Controlling Process Group
   - Monitor and Control Project Work Process
   - Perform Integrated Change Control Process
   - Verify Scope Process
   - Control Scope Process
   - Control Schedule Process
   - Control Cost Process
   - Quality Control Process
   - Performance Reporting Process
   - Risk Monitoring and Control Process
   - Procurement Administration Process

5. Closing Process Group
   - Phase of Project Closure Process
   - Procurement Closure Process

The following discussion will not take a deeper, more detailed look at each of the Project Management Process groups and their associated processes.

Questions to Consider

1. How is the performance of your organizations current approach to project management as well as the performance of the phases currently used in your project management method evaluated?
2. What is the relationship between the Project Management Process Groups profiled here and the project management phases your organization currently applies to projects it is engaged in?
3. How could these Project Management Process Groups be integrated into your current project management methodology?
4. How could this work enhance project risk management in your organization?
5. How would such an integration enhance your organizations project management overall performance and impact on client service delivery?

Initiating Process Group

As the title says the Initiation Process Group is comprised of the processes required to define a new project or to gain the authorization required to start another phase of an existing project. In the context of this work the initial project scope is defined and the initial financial resources are allocated and committed. This work also includes the internal and external stakeholders, those individuals and groups who can or will be impacted and who have some say or influence in overall project execution and performance, are identified. The project manager will be assigned at this point, if it has not been done already. All project information generated to this point is captured in the project charter and stakeholder register.

The Initiating Process Group may also have responsibility for breaking projects into separate and distinct phases at this point as well. This allows large projects to be "chunked" in ways that make them more understandable and manageable. This also helps to manager risk by allowing for small issues and problems to be caught early, before they are able to cause damage to the project or its ability to execute and deliver.

As mentioned earlier, process activities can be repeated throughout the project life-cycle. This applies here as well. By cycling through initiating processes in subsequent phases the decisions involved with developing the project charter and identifying stakeholders can be reviewed and validated. The success criteria associated with overall project execution and client service delivery are validated. The influence of stakeholders as well as internal and external factors can also be reviewed. This work allows a more informed decision to be made regarding project continuation, delay, or ending.

It is important to ensure customers and stakeholders are included in the initiation stage. It helps to improve the likelihood and impact of shared ownership, acceptance of deliverables, and overall stakeholder and customer satisfaction. The Initiating Process Group is comprised of the following project management processes:

1. Develop Project Charter – focuses on the work associated with developing the document that formally authorizes a project or project phase.

Also documents the initiation requirements to the satisfaction of the stakeholders. In multi-phase projects this process can be used to validate or refine the decisions made during the previous review and iteration of the project charter. Inputs required for this process:

- Project statement of work
- Business case
- Contract
- Enterprise environmental factors
- Organizational process assets

2. Identify Stakeholders – as we have discussed, stakeholders bring a variety of different perspectives to the project. Some stakeholders will be necessary for project success and will be positively impacted by the project and what it delivers. Others will not be needed or be critical to the success of the project but will also be positively impacted by the results. A third group of stakeholders will be needed for success but will be negatively impacted in some form or fashion while a fourth group will also be negatively impacted but will not be essential to overall project execution and client service delivery. Inputs required in support of the stakeholder identification process include:

- Project charter
- Procurement documents
- Enterprise environmental factors
- Organizational process assets

Questions to Consider

1. How are projects currently initiated in your organization?
2. What types of tools, methods and processes are used in support of initiation?
3. What role does the business case play in project initiation in your organization?
4. How are the potentially multiple groups of stakeholders identified in the context of the initiation of a specific project in your organization?
5. How are the needs of these potentially multiple groups of stakeholders addressed during the initiation process in your organization?
6. What types of enterprise environmental factors does your organization address when initiating a project?
7. How does your organization address enterprise environmental factors when initiating a project?
8. What types of organizational process assets does your organization address when initiating a project?
9. How does your organization address these assets when initiating a project?
10. What role does a project charter play in your organizations project management processes?
11. How is the effectiveness and impact of your organizations current practices in these areas evaluated?
12. What is the current state of your organizations performance in these areas?
13. What are the opportunities for improvement in these areas?

14. How would improvement in these areas enhance your organizations project management and execution as well as overall client service delivery?

Planning Process Group

This group consists of the processes that need to be performed to establish and ensure understanding of the total scope of the effort, define the project objectives and then refine them, and then define the course of action required to achieve those objectives. The planning processes result in the development of the project management plan and the project documents. This material will provide the guidelines supporting overall successful project execution. Because projects are based on successive iterations there will be consistent feedback loops that allow for information to be consistently reviewed throughout the project. Additional information may also drive the need for additional planning work to ensure project execution remains aligned with stakeholders, environmental factors, etc. This method of progressive and continuous detailing and refining of the project management plan is sometimes referred to as "rolling wave planning". This reflects the idea that planning and documentation are iterative and on-going throughout the project life-cycle. The Planning Process Group consists of twenty specific project management processes. This is far more processes than any of the other Process Groups. The reason is obvious to anyone who has been involved with projects. Planning is the cornerstone for any successful initiative. Effective and comprehensive planning goes a long way to ensuring the right things are done when they need to be done in the manner in which they need to be done. The specific project management processes supporting the Project Planning Process Group are:

1. Develop Project Management Plan – this work involves the process of defining, preparing, integrating and coordinating the project management plan and all supporting, subordinate and associated plans. The project management plan is the primary source of information on how the project will be planned, executed, monitored, evaluated, controlled and closed. Key inputs supporting development of the project management plan:
    *   Project charter
    *   Outputs from other associated and supporting planning processes
    *   Enterprise environmental factors
    *   Organizational process assets

2. Collect Requirements – this process focuses on identifying, defining and documenting the stakeholder needs that need to be met in order for the project objectives to be satisfied. An important point to keep in mind that as mentioned earlier, stakeholders and stakeholder groups are not created equally. They bring different needs and perspectives to the project. Understanding these needs is critical to overall project success. Key inputs supporting collection of requirements include and creation of associated requirements documentation include:
    *   Project charter
    *   Stakeholder register

118

3. Define Scope – scope definition is the process of developing a detailed description of the project and product. Key inputs supporting the creation of the project scope statement and project document updates include:
   - Project charter
   - Project requirements documentation
   - Organizational process assets

4. Create Work Break Down Structure (WBS) – the work break down structure is a detailed listing of all of the activities associated with completing required project deliverables and successful project execution. The WBS approach allows large areas of work to be broken down into manageable elements that can be scheduled and assigned. Key inputs leading to the creation of the WBS, WBS dictionary, scope baseline, and updates to project documents include:
   - Project scope statement
   - Project requirements documentation
   - Organizational process assets

5. Define Activities – activities definition is the process of identifying the specific actions that need to be performed to produce the project deliverables and required outcomes. Key inputs leading to and supporting the creation and maintenance of the activity list, activity attributes and milestone list include:
   - Project scope baseline
   - Enterprise environmental factors
   - Organizational process assets

6. Sequence Activities – this work involves the process of identifying and documenting the relationships among the project activities. Key inputs supporting the creation of the project schedule network diagrams and project document updates include:
   - Activity list
   - Activity attributes
   - Milestone list
   - Project scope statement
   - Organizational process assets

7. Estimate Activity Resources – this is the process of estimating the type, quantity and quality of material, people, equipment, supplies and resources required to perform each project related activity. Key inputs support this work and the creation of the activity resource requirements documentation, resource break down structure, and project documentation updates include:
   - Activity list
   - Activity attributes
   - Resource calendars
   - Enterprise environmental factors
   - Organizational process assets

8. Estimate Activity Durations – activity duration is the amount of time required to complete a specific set of work related actions. The process of activity duration estimation focuses on determining the amount of time required to complete individual project activities along with the amount and type of resources requires. The

inputs required to generate the activity duration estimates and project updates include:

- Activity list
- Activity attributes
- Activity resource requirements
- Resource calendars
- Project scope statement
- Enterprise environmental factors
- Organizational process assets

9. Develop Schedule – this project management process involves analyzing activity sequences, durations, resource requirements, and schedule constraints needed to create the project schedule. Inputs required to support the creation and maintenance of the project schedule, project schedule baseline, schedule data and updates to project documents include:

- Activity list
- Activity attributes
- Project schedule network diagrams
- Activity resource requirements
- Resource calendars
- Activity duration estimates
- Project scope statement
- Enterprise environmental factors
- Organizational processes assets

10. Estimate Costs – this work involves developing an approximation of the funding needed to complete the identified project activities. Inputs required to produce the activity cost estimates,

basis of estimates and updates to project documents include:

- Scope baseline
- Project schedule
- Human resource plan
- Risk register
- Enterprise environmental factors
- Organizational process assets

11. Determine Budget – this is the process of aggregating the estimated costs of individual activities or work packages to establish an authorized cost baseline. Inputs required to produce the cost performance baseline, project funding requirements, and updates to project documents include:
    - Activity cost estimates
    - Basis of estimates
    - Scope baseline
    - Project schedule
    - Resource calendars
    - Contracts
    - Organizational process assets

12. Plan for Quality – work associated with this process area focuses on identifying the quality requirements and / or standards needed by the project or product as well as documenting how the project will demonstrate compliance with these requirements. Inputs required to produce the project quality management plan, quality metrics, quality checklists, process improvement plan and updates to project documentation include:

- Scope baseline
- Stakeholder register
- Cost performance baseline
- Risk register
- Enterprise environmental factors
- Organizational process assets

13. Develop Human Resource Plan – this process supports the identification and documentation of project roles, responsibilities and required skills, reporting relationships. It also supports the development of a staffing management plan. Inputs required to produce the project human resource plan include:
- Activity resource requirements
- Enterprise environmental factors
- Organizational process assets

14. Plan Communications – work associated with and in support of this project management process focuses on determining and documenting stakeholder information and communication needs as well as defining a communication approach for the project. Inputs required to produce the project communication plan as well as support the updating of project management documentation include:
- Stakeholder register
- Stakeholder management strategy
- Enterprise environmental factors
- Organizational processes assets

15. Plan Risk Management – this project management process focuses on identifying and

defining how to conduct risk management activities in support of project management and execution as well as overall client service delivery. Inputs required to produce and support the project risk management plan include:

- Project scope statement
- Cost management plan
- Schedule management plan
- Communications management plan
- Enterprise environmental factors
- Organizational process assets

16. Identify Risks – work associated with risk identification focuses on determining which risks may affect the project, the extent to which they could affect as well as their potential impact, and documenting the specific characteristics of each risk. Inputs required to produce the project risk register include:

- Risk management plan
- Activity cost estimates
- Activity duration estimates
- Project scope baseline
- Stakeholder register
- Cost management plan
- Schedule management plan
- Quality management plan
- Enterprise environmental factors
- Organizational process assets

17. Perform Qualitative Risk Analysis – qualitative risk analysis is the process of prioritizing real and potential risks to the project allowing for further

analysis and action. The work focuses on analyzing and understanding the probability of occurrence combined with the likelihood of occurrence. Inputs required to support updates to the risk register through the project life-cycle include:

- Risk register
- Risk management plan
- Project scope statement
- Organizational process assets

18. Perform Quantitative Risk Analysis – work on this project process focuses on the numerical analysis of the real or potential effect of identified risks on the ability of the project to deliver on identified objectives. Inputs required to support updates to the risk register throughout the project life-cycle include:

- Risk register
- Risk management plan
- Cost management plan
- Schedule management plan
- Organizational process assets

19. Plan Risk Responses – this work focuses on developing options and actions to enhance opportunities and to reduce threats to project objectives, project performance and overall client service delivery. Inputs required to produce updates to the risk register throughout the project life-cycle, risk related contract decisions, updates to the project management plan, and updates to associated project documentation plan include:

- Risk register

- Risk management plan

20. Plan Procurements – work associated with and in support of this project management process focuses on the documentation of purchasing and procurement decisions, specifying the processes and approaches that will be used in support of procurement as well as identifying potential vendors that can support project needs. Inputs required to produce the project procurement management plan, procurement statements of work, make or buy decisions, project procurement documents, source selection criteria, and change requests include:
    - Project scope baseline
    - Requirements documentation
    - Teaming agreements
    - Risk register
    - Risk related contract decisions
    - Activity resource requirements
    - Project schedule
    - Activity cost estimates
    - Cost performance baseline
    - Enterprise environmental factors
    - Organizational process assets

As mentioned, the planning process group contains the largest number (20) of project management processes. Why? Because planning lays the foundation for project execution. The quality of work done here plays a major role in the quality of work done in the next area, execution. It is also important to keep in mind that the next phase consumes the majority of resources allocated for the project. Proper planning will help to ensure the resources are used in the

126

most efficient, effective manner required for successful project execution and overall client service delivery.

Questions to Consider

1. How does your organization currently approach the work associated with the development of the project management plan?
2. How are the project charter, planning processes, enterprise environmental factors and organizational process assets leveraged in work associated with and in support of the development of the project management plan?
3. How does your organization currently approach the work associated with collecting requirements in support of projects?
4. What tools, methods and processes are used to collect requirements?
5. What sources are used in the process of collecting requirements in support of projects your organization is involved in?
6. How is the scope of projects your organization is involved in defined?
7. What tools, methods are processes are used in the process of scope definition?
8. What information sources are used to support and validate the scope of projects your organization is involved in?
9. What types of tools, methods, and processes are used to create the project Work Break Down Structure (WBS) or other associated program documents?

10. What information sources are used to support and validate the information and approach profiled in the WBS?
11. How are the activities associated with successful project performance defined in projects your organization is involved with?
12. What tools, methods are processes are used when defining activities?
13. What information and data sources are used to define activities in support of projects?
14. What methods, tools and processes are used to sequence activities in support of project planning?
15. What information and data sources are used in support of activity sequencing?
16. What tools, methods and processes are used when estimating resources required in support of project related activities?
17. What resources are identified as required for successful project execution?
18. What information and data sources are used in support of activity resource estimating?
19. How does your organization develop schedules in support of projects it is involved in?
20. What tools, methods and processes are used in support of project schedule development?
21. What information and data sources are used in support of schedule development?
22. What does your organization consider to fall into the cost category in the context of project execution?
23. How does your organization estimate costs associated with projects it is involved in?
24. What tools, methods and processes are used in support of project cost estimation?

25. What information and data sources are used in support of project cost estimation?
26. What items are included when building a budget in support of projects your organization is involved in?
27. What tools, methods and processes are used in support of project budget development?
28. What information and data sources are used when creating a project budget in your organization?
29. How does your organization define quality in the context of project design, planning and execution?
30. What are the critical quality attributes your organization strives for in the context of project execution and client service delivery?
31. What tools, methods are processes are used to define quality attributes and then integrate these attributes into the project planning process?
32. What information and data sources are leveraged in support of planning quality in support of projects your organization engages in?
33. How are human resourcing needs addressed when planning projects in your organization?
34. Which tools, methods and processes are used in support of identifying and developing the human resource plan in support of the project?
35. Where are personnel required to support projects drawn from?
36. What core competencies are project personnel expected to bring to a project team?
37. Which competencies is the project team prepared to support project personnel in acquiring?
38. How does your organization enable and support the team members in the acquisition and

development of competencies required for
successful project execution and client service
delivery?

39. Which tools, methods and processes does your
organization use to identify the communication
needs associated with and in support of projects it
is involved in?

40. How does your organization identify the
communication needs associated with projects the
organization is involved with?

41. How does the organization identify the
communication needs of the various client,
stakeholder, and supplier groups that are involved
with and support projects your organization is
involved with?

42. How does your organization fulfill the
communication needs of those who are interested
in, involved with, or impacted by projects the
organization is involved in?

43. Which tools, methods are processes does your
organization use to identify the risks associated
with projects it is involved with?

44. How are these risks evaluated?

45. How are these risks mitigated?

46. How is the effectiveness of risk mitigation
evaluated from a qualitative perspective?

47. How is the effectiveness of risk mitigation
evaluated from a quantitative perspective?

48. What methods, tools, and processes are used to
identify appropriate risk responses in support of
projects your organization is involved in?

49. How are selected risk responses tested?

50. How are the results of risk response testing evaluated in the context of projects your organization is involved with or supporting?
51. What tools, methods and processes does your organization use to plan procurement activities in support of projects it is involved with?
52. How are potential suppliers identified?
53. How are potential suppliers selected?
54. How are selected suppliers managed?
55. How is the performance of selected suppliers evaluated?
56. How are the results of work associated with overall project planning your organization is involved in validated?
57. How is the effectiveness of the work associated with and in support of project planning in your organization currently evaluated?
58. How effective are the current methods, processes and tools in terms of their impact on overall project execution and client service delivery?
59. What are the opportunities for improvement in the area of project planning in your organization?
60. How would improvement in this area impact overall project execution and client service delivery?

Executing Process Group

The Executing Process Group encompasses the processes performed to complete the work defined in the project management plan in support of and to satisfy the project specifications. This process group supports and enhances the coordination of people and resources in the most efficient and effective manner possible to achieve the

131

project objectives. It helps to ensure this work is accomplished within the context, guidelines and intent of the project management plan.

As mentioned previously, projects are iterative in nature. As projects progress successive project steps build upon previous work. In addition, as the project moves along changes in the client service delivery environment, project performance environment, etc. can drive the need for on-going planning updates and even re-baselining. Events in this space can include changes to anticipated activity durations, changes in resource productivity and availability, as well as unanticipated risks. These variances can affect the project management plan and project documents. It may also drive change requests that if approved could modify the project management plan and even drive the need to establish new project performance baselines. As mentioned, it is also important to keep in mind that project execution is where the vast majority of the people, money, time and resources that have been allocated to the project are going to be spent. Solid execution will play a major role in helping to ensure those resources are expended effectively and efficiently. The following processes comprise the Executing Process Group.

1. Direct and Manage Project Execution – this project management process is focused on the performance of the work specified in the project management plan, specifically the work designed to achieve the project objectives. Process inputs required to provide required project deliverables, work performance information, change requests, updates to the project management plan and project documentation include:
    • Project management plan

132

- Approved change requests
- Enterprise environmental factors
- Organizational process assets

2. Perform Quality Assurance – this is the process of auditing the quality requirements and the results from quality control measurements and assessments. This work is designed to ensure quality standards and expectations are being met. Inputs required to support updates to organizational process assets, change requests, updates to the project management plan and documentation include:
   - Project management plan
   - Quality metrics
   - Work performance information
   - Quality control measurements

3. Acquire Project Team – this work focuses on the process of confirming the availability and quality of qualified personnel and then obtaining the team needed to complete project assignments. Inputs required to provide proper project staff assignments, resource calendars, and updates the project management plan include:
   - Project management plan
   - Enterprise environmental factors
   - Organizational process assets

4. Develop Project Team – this activity focuses on improving the competencies, team interaction and the overall team environment to enhance project performance. Inputs required to produce and

support team performance assessments and enterprise environmental factors updates include:

- Project staff assignments
- Project management plan
- Resource calendars

5. Manage Project Team – work associated with this process involves tracking team member performance, providing feedback, resolving issues, and managing changes to maximize project performance. Input required in support of updating enterprise environmental factors and organizational process assets, change requests, and updates to the project management plan include:

- Project staff assignments
- Project management plan
- Team performance assessments
- Performance reports
- Organizational process assets

6. Distribute Information – work here involves the process of making relevant and required information available to project stakeholders. Inputs required to ensure timely and accurate updates to organizational process assets includes:

- Project management plan
- Performance reports
- Organizational process assets

7. Manage Stakeholder Expectations – this work focuses on communicating to and working with stakeholders. The goal is to meet their needs in the context of project execution and overall client

service delivery. Proactively identifying and addressing needs is a major part of this work. Inputs required to ensure timely and accurate updates to organizational process assets, project management plans and documents as well as change requests include:

- Stakeholder register
- Stakeholder management strategy
- Project management plan
- Issue log
- Change log
- Organizational process assets

8. Conduct Procurements – this project process work supports creation and distribution of requests for proposals, obtaining and screening vendor responses, selecting appropriate vendors based on agreed upon criteria, contract award and management. Process inputs required to create the requests for proposals, identifying and selecting vendors, create and maintain resource calendars, manage change requests, update project management plans and project documents include:

- Project management plan
- Procurement documents
- Source selection criteria
- Qualified seller list
- Seller proposals
- Project documents
- Make or buy decisions
- Teaming agreements
- Organizational process assets

Once execution on project tasks and activities has begun, they must be monitored and controlled to ensure project and client service delivery are being maintained within the agreed upon time-lines, cost controls, and quality specifications.

Questions to Consider

1. What methods, tools and processes does your organization use to direct and manage projects and overall client service delivery?
2. How is the effectiveness of the application of these methods, tools and processes evaluated?
3. How is the information and data gained from these evaluations integrated into the overall process of client execution and client service delivery?
4. What methods, tools and processes are used to perform quality assurance activities associated with and in support of project execution and client service delivery?
5. Where is the work associated with quality assurance placed within the project management framework? For example, who do the people responsible for quality assurance report to in the project management structure? What is the frequency of their reviews and reporting? What is the scope of their responsibilities?
6. How are the competencies associated with successful project performance identified? Specific competency areas include technical, business, leadership and management.

7. How are personnel selected for project assignments based on these competencies?
8. How are personnel indoctrinated into their project roles?
9. What type of support is available to them to enable them to perform in their roles effectively?
10. What methods, tools and processes are used to evaluate the effectiveness of the means used to identify, select and assign project personnel?
11. What methods, tools and processes are used to develop both the team and the members comprising the team once it is in place?
12. What methods, tools and processes are used to evaluate the effectiveness of this development and its impact on overall project performance and client service delivery?
13. What methods, tools and processes are used to manage the performance of the project team as a whole and individuals once the project work is underway?
14. How are performance expectations for team members identified and communicated?
15. How are team members provided with the resources they need to perform in their roles effectively?
16. How is feedback leveraged to enhance and sustain the performance of members of the project team?
17. How is the relationship of the project to the larger organizational objectives communicated and reinforced to members of the project team, stakeholders, suppliers, and other who are or may be impacted by the project?
18. How is the effectiveness of these methods, tools and processes evaluated?

19. What methods, tools and processes are used to collect, analyze and distribute information and communication to project team members, stakeholder groups, suppliers, and other interested parties?
20. How is the effectiveness and impact of this work on overall project execution and client service delivery evaluated?
21. What methods, tools and processes are used to identify project stakeholders?
22. How are stakeholders differentiated, e.g., those who support and will be positively impacted, those who support and will be negative impacted, those who do not support and will be positively impacted, those who do not support and will be negatively impacted, etc.?
23. How is the effectiveness of stakeholder identification and management methods, processes and tools evaluated in the context of its impact on overall project execution and client service delivery?
24. What tools, methods are processes are used to conduct procurements in support of project execution?
25. How is the effectiveness of these tools, methods and processes evaluated?
26. What are the opportunities for improvement in the areas of directing the project, quality assurance, project team acquisition, project team development, management of the project team, information distribution, stakeholder management, and procurement management?

27. How would improvement in these areas impact overall project execution and client service delivery?

Monitoring and Controlling Process Group

This Process Group is comprised of the project processes required to track, review, and regulate the progress and performance of the project. This work also allows project team members to identify areas requiring changes to the plan and to initiate work supporting those changes. The primary benefit of the work associated with and in support of this Process Group is that project performance and progress is monitored and measured regularly and consistently. This allows variances from the project management plan to be identified, tracked, evaluated and controlled.

There are additional benefits to this Process Group. These include change control, preventive action, and managing and influencing factors that could circumvent the goal of integrated change control. This discipline and rigor allows for and supports only those changes that have been reviewed and approved in being implemented.

The activities associated with and in support of project monitoring and controlling continue throughout the project event. This continuous attention provides the project team with insight into the health of the project. It also allows areas requiring attention to be identified as early as possible, in many cases long before they can cause real problems with the project or overall client service delivery. An additional benefit is based on the fact that the processes associated with monitoring and controlling look at both individual elements of project execution and client service delivery as well as a

139

holistic, systematic perspective. The result of this level of comprehensive oversight allows for changes to the project plan to be made from the perspective of the total project. This reduces the risk of correcting a problem or issue in one area only to create one in another.

The following processes make up the Monitoring and Controlling Process Group:

1. Monitor and control project work – work associated with this area includes tracking, reviewing and regulating the progress of the project to meet the performance objectives defined in the project management plan. Monitoring includes status reporting, progress measurement and forecasting. Performance reports provide information on project performance in the area of scope, schedule, cost, resources, quality and risk. As with all data collected throughout the project it is important to keep in mind that it can be used where needed across the project event. Inputs required in support of the development and delivery of change requests, and updates to the project management plan and other project documents include:

   • Project management plan
   • Performance reports
   • Enterprise environmental factors
   • Organizational process assets

2. Perform integrated change control – this work involves reviewing all change requests,

140

approving changes and managing changes to deliverables, organizational process assets, project documents and the project management plan. Inputs required to support the delivery and maintenance of updates to change request status, project management plan and project documentation include:

- Project management plan
- Work performance information
- Change requests
- Enterprise environmental factors
- Organizational process assets

3. Verify scope – the process of formalizing acceptance of project deliverables that have been completed. Inputs required to support the development and delivery of required deliverables, change requests and updates to project management documents include:
   - Project management plan
   - Requirements documentation
   - Requirements traceability matrix
   - Validated deliverables

4. Control scope work associated with this process involves monitoring the status of the project and product scope and managing changes to the scope baseline. Inputs required in support of work performance measurements and change requests as well as updates to organizational process assets, the project management plan and project document updates include:

- Project management plan
- Work performance information
- Requirements documentation
- Requirements traceability matrix
- Organizational process assets

5. Control schedule – this work focuses on the process of monitoring the status of the project to update project progress and managing changes to the schedule baseline. Inputs required to support the delivery and maintenance of work performance measurements and change requests as well as updates to organizational process assets, project management plan and project documentation include:
   - Project management plan
   - Project schedule
   - Work performance information
   - Organizational process assets

6. Control costs – this is the process of monitoring the status of the project to update the project budget and managing changes to the cost baseline. Inputs required to support the delivery and maintenance of work performance measurements, budget forecasts and change requests as well as updates to organizational process assets, project management plan and project documentation include:
   - Project management plan
   - Project funding requirements
   - Work performance information

142

- Organizational process assets

7. Perform quality control – work in this area focuses on monitoring and recording results of executing the quality activities to assess project performance and recommend any needed changes. Inputs required to support the delivery and maintenance of quality control measurements, validated changes, validated deliverables, and change requests as well as updates to organizational process assets, project management plan and project documentation include:
   - Project management plan
   - Quality metrics
   - Quality checklists
   - Work performance measurements
   - Approved change requests
   - Identified deliverables
   - Organizational process assets

8. Report performance – work in this process group area focuses on collecting and distributing project performance information. This information can include status reports, progress measurements, and forecasts. Inputs required to support the delivery and maintenance of updates to risk registers, organizational process assets, project management plan and project management documentation as well as change requests include:
   - Risk register
   - Project management plan

- Work performance information
- Performance reports

9. Monitor and control risk – the process of implementing risk response plans, tracking identified risks, monitoring residual risks, identifying new risks, and evaluating the effectiveness of risk management processes throughout the project life-cycle. Inputs required to produce and maintain change requests as well as updates to risk registers, organizational process updates, project management plans, and project documentation include:
   - Risk register
   - Project management plan
   - Work performance information
   - Performance reports

10. Administer procurements – procurement administration focuses on managing procurement relationships, monitoring contract performance, and making changes and corrections as needed. Inputs required to produce and maintain procurement documentation and change requests as well as updates to organizational process assets and project management planning documents include:
    - Procurement documentation
    - Project management plan
    - Contracts
    - Performance reports
    - Approved change requests
    - Work performance information

To this point we have examined four of the Project Management Process Groups, specifically Initiation, Planning, Executing, and Monitoring and Controlling. The final Project Management Process Control Group focuses on closing the project.

Questions to Consider

1. What methods, tools and processes are used to monitor and control project work across all phases and areas of activities?
2. How is the effectiveness of these methods, tools, and processes evaluated?
3. What methods, tools, and processes are used to perform, manage and support integrated change control across the project life-cycle?
4. How is the effectiveness of these methods, tools and processes evaluated?
5. What methods, tools and processes are used to verify project scope?
6. When is the scope of a project event considered locked and not subject to any additional change?
7. What factors are considered when locking in project scope?
8. How are the elements of speed, cost, quality and risk factored into this analysis and ultimate decision?
9. How is the effectiveness of the methods, tools and processes associated with scope verification and management evaluated?
10. What methods, tools and processes are used to support project schedule control?

11. How are stakeholder expectations managed in the context of schedule control, in particular on projects when planning work consumes what appears to be a larger than normal part of the schedule?
12. How is the effectiveness of these methods, tools and processes evaluated?
13. What methods, tools, and processes are used to track, manage and control costs associated with overall project execution and client service delivery?
14. How are stakeholder expectations managed in the context of cost control, in particular on projects when planning work consumes what appears to be a larger than normal portion of the budget?
15. How is the effectiveness of these methods, tools and processes evaluated?
16. What methods, tools and processes are used to perform quality control?
17. Which members of the project team are given responsibility for quality control?
18. How are members of the project team assigned to perform quality control roles selected?
19. How are members of the project team assigned to quality control roles provided the resources and support they need to effectively fulfill these roles?
20. How is the effectiveness of these methods, tools and processes evaluated?
21. What tools, methods and processes are used to report project performance?
22. Who is this information provided to?
23. What is the frequency of communication?
24. How is the information differentiated among various stakeholder groups, suppliers, etc.?

25. How is the effectiveness of the methods, tools and processes associated with this work evaluated?
26. What methods, tools, and processes are used to monitor and control risks once the project is underway?
27. How are risks identified once the project is underway correlated back to the risk analysis that was performed at the beginning of the event?
28. How are differences in the two sets of information reconciled?
29. Who on the project team is given responsibilities associated with monitoring and controlling risks?
30. How are these personnel selected?
31. How are personnel performing in these roles provided the resources and support they need to perform these roles effectively?
32. How are risk updates communicated to project team members, stakeholders, suppliers, etc.?
33. How is the effectiveness of the methods, tools and processes associated with this work evaluated?
34. What methods, tools and processes are used to administer procurements across the project lifecycle?
35. How are project resourcing and support needs identified?
36. How are requests for proposals vetted within the organization before they are submitted to potential suppliers for review and bid?
37. How are potential vendors vetted?
38. What criteria are used for vendor selection?
39. How are these criteria identified?
40. How are these criteria communicated?
41. How are vendors ultimately selected?

42. How are vendors initially engaged in the work associated with the project?
43. Who oversees the quality of the products and services the vendor provides?
44. How is the effectiveness of the methods, tools and processes associated with this work evaluated?
45. What are the opportunities for improvement in the areas monitoring and controlling project work, change control, scope verification, scope control, schedule control, cost control, quality control, performance reporting, risk monitoring and control and procurement administration?
46. How would improvement in these areas impact overall project execution and client service delivery?

Closing Process Group

As you can see and may well have experienced, projects can consume large amounts of resources as well as the time and energy of people who work on them. After getting through all of the work associated with and in support of delivering on the commitments laid out in the project plan it would be natural to want to consider the work finished. To do so however would be a mistake. Unfortunately this mistake is made on some project events. It is critically important to close a project properly. Failure to do so means the project is not really complete.

The Closing Process Group is comprised of the processes required to finalize all activities across all Project Management Process Groups. Doing this ensures that all obligations associated with project, client, phase or contractual obligations and fulfilled and closed properly.

When completed, the work associated with this Process Group verifies and validates that the defined processes with all Process Groups have been completed, fulfilled and closed properly. Specific outcomes can include:

- Sponsor or client acceptance
- Post-project or end phase review
- Documenting any impacts resulting from tailoring of specific processes
- Documenting lessons learned
- Required updates to organizational process assets
- Documentation archiving
- Procurement close-out

The Closing Process Group consists of the following process group project management processes.

1. Close project or phase – work in this area focuses on finalizing all activities across all of the preceding Project Management Process Groups. Doing this formally closes the specific phase being addressed or the project as a whole. Inputs required to produce the final product, service or result transition to closure and updates to organizational process assets include:
   - Project management plan
   - Accepted deliverables
   - Organizational process assets

2. Close procurement – this work focuses on completing all procurement activity associated with and in support of the project. Inputs required

149

to support procurement closure and updates to organizational process assets include:
- Project management plan
- Procurement documentation

This discussion has profiled the five Project Management Process Groups as defined by PMI. Those groups are Initiate, Plan, Execute, Monitor and Control and Close. When applied in total they support a structured, more predictable and disciplined approach to project execution and management. This level of rigor helps to reduce the uncertainty projects can generate.

Questions to Consider

1. What methods, tools and processes does your organization use to close projects or project phases?
2. Who is involved with project or phase closure?
3. What activities are associated with project or phase closure?
4. How is the effectiveness of the methods, tools and processes associated with this work evaluated?
5. What methods, tools and processes are used to close procurements associated with or in support of project or phase activities?
6. How is the effectiveness of these methods, tools and processes evaluated?
7. What are the opportunities for improvement in these areas?
8. How would improvement in these areas enhance overall project execution and client service delivery?

Project Management Knowledge Areas

Overview

We have now finished examining the five Project Management Process Groups and their associated processes. The Project Management Institute (PMI) also organizes the learning and work associated with project execution and client service delivery based on specific knowledge areas. This enables personnel associated with projects to focus both on the project as a whole as well as specific areas they may be involved in and responsible for. The following profiles the 9 PMI   Knowledge Areas along with their corresponding project management processes.

The Nine PMI Project Management Areas of Knowledge

1. Project Integration Management
   - Project Charter Development Process
   - Project Management Plan Development Process
   - Project Direction and Execution Management Process
   - Project Work Monitoring and Controlling Process
   - Integrated Change Control Process
   - Phase or Project Closure Process

2. Project Scope Management
   - Requirements Collection Process
   - Scope Definition Process
   - Work Break Down Structure Creation Process
   - Scope Verification Process
   - Scope Control Process

3. Project Time Management
   - Activities Definition Process
   - Activities Sequencing Process
   - Activity Resources Estimation Process
   - Activity Duration Estimation Process
   - Schedule Development Process
   - Schedule Control Process

4. Project Cost Management
   - Cost Estimating Process
   - Budget Determination Process
   - Cost Control Process

5. Project Quality Management
   - Quality Planning Process
   - Quality Assurance Process
   - Quality Control Process

6. Project Human Resource Management
   - Human Resource Plan Development Process
   - Project Team Acquisition Process
   - Project Team Management Process

7. Project Communications Management
   - Stakeholder Identification Process
   - Communication Planning Process
   - Information Distribution Process
   - Stakeholder Expectation Management Process
   - Performance Reporting Process

8. Project Risk Management

- Risk Management Planning Process
- Risk Identification Process
- Quantitative Risk Analysis Process
- Qualitative Risk Analysis Process
- Risk Response Planning Process
- Risk Monitoring and Control Process

9. Project Procurement Management
   - Procurement Planning Process
   - Procurement Performance Process
   - Procurement Administration Process
   - Procurement Closure Process

A Primer on Agile Development

Introduction

Agile project management is traditionally aligned with software development. Software development is a merging of science and art. It is a science based on its use of mathematical models and other types of scientific tools. It is an art based on the idea that even though they are presented with the same problem, different developers can come up with radically different solutions, not only in terms of how the application performs but also the use of different programming languages to create and implement the solution.

Agile came into existence based on the belief of practitioners that other project management models were not sufficient in enabling teams to deliver. Unlike some other project management methods, Agile seeks to leverage the members of the team by creating and sustaining a performance environment characterized by empowerment and trust, acknowledging and accepting that change is the norm, and promoting continuous feedback.

Based on the history of project management, from approximately 1900 to roughly 1980 project management activities focused on the identification and allocation of people, time, money and material in the most efficient manner possible to achieve the target outcomes. It is no coincidence that project management and the tasks associated with it took on a highly pragmatic, measurement based focus that reflected the best of Frederick Taylor and Scientific Management.

It is also not surprising that the Agile philosophy and approach to Project Management came into being around

159

1980. This was the time where the PC and associated software development industry was beginning to take root.

Initially, traditional project management methods, e.g., phased, milestone, incremental or waterfall were tried. However, as developers quickly discovered designing software is not like building a bridge. Bridge building is more or less a static exercise. Once the design is set it does not and in fact cannot change. The bridge must meet or exceed a very specific set of functional attributes. These include the ability to handle a certain amount of traffic and to withstand weather conditions. There is another set of attributes, known as quality attributes, that focus on the visual or aesthetic appeal of the of the span. These include things like color, lighting (non-safety related), etc. While important, these non-functional characteristics are for the most part a distant second to the ability of the bridge to carry traffic safely for many years, even decades.

As the designers and architects of early software discovered, their trade had to look at both functional and quality attributes in an equal light. They also found that unlike steel work, whose methods, practices and tools have remained consistent for well over 100 years, the methods, technologies and tools associated with and in support of software development were (and still are) constantly evolving. This level of change was and continues to be characteristic of the clients that are being supported as well. This level of change means that client requirements can change literally overnight.

This brings us back to a point we made earlier, that being software development is as much art as science involving as much innovation and creativity as pragmatism.

160

Software cannot be created on an assembly line or stamped out in a factory in a factory.

The processes associated with and in support of Agile are not new. Teams have been developing small, frequent releases, worked in pairs, and getting close to their customers for years. What is different about Agile is that it is now mature enough to allow the practices to be taught, learned, adopted, and applied on a scale of the organizations choosing.

The Agile Methodologies

When something is not working to the level people need or expect it to they will look for alternatives. Such is the case with project management as well.

"Agile" is an umbrella term used to describe a specific set of software development methodologies. As such Agile software development and the supporting / enabling project management methods and tools represent a set of fundamentals and principles that focus on the best way to develop software. This group of methodologies includes:

- Adaptive Software Development (ASD)
- The Crystal Methodologies
- Dynamic Systems Development Method (DSDM)
- Extreme Programming (XP)
- Feature Driven Development (FDD)
- Lean Software Development
- Scrum

Each of these methodologies shares the Agile philosophy of being close and responsive to the customer.

The difference comes in terms of how each approaches the task of software development. For example Scrum and ASD ate highly focused on the management of the development process as well as communication between developers and customers. On the other XP is clearly focused on programming practices. FDD focuses on clearly defining the processes the development team should follow. Crystal advocates the idea of having tailored processes for every project.

What these examples highlight is that Agile software development and the project management tools and methods that support it focus on matching the project management method with the needs of the project. This represents a major change from the days of "waterfall", "milestone", or more traditional approaches to project management and project enabled client service delivery, where outcomes sometimes took a back seat to process.

The Agile Manifesto, Agile Values and Agile Principles

As a mindset Agile has been around since the 1980's. However, it wasn't until 2001 that the mindset, values and practices associated with and in support of Agile crystalized to the point where they began to gain real traction in the software development project management environment.

It was in 2001 that the Agile Manifesto was first published. At the core of the manifesto and of Agile itself is the idea that facilitating change is far more effective than attempting to prevent it. It is better to develop and trust in your ability as well as that of your team to respond to unpredictable events than it is to trust in your ability to plan

162

for and cope with disaster. Put another way, Agile is nothing more than what happens when a project goes critical. When this happens all of the activities that once seemed so important, like certain types of documentation, meetings, etc. take a back seat to client service delivery. Agile simply puts the importance of client service delivery, based on the idea that a project is initiated to provide a specific deliverable, right up front.

The manifesto puts forward the following values:

- Place importance and focus on individuals and interactions over processes and tools. This means Agile places a premium on software development professionals. The success of any development effort is going to be based on the competencies, effort and action of the members of the team. A critical element of the success of a software development team is found in its ability to correctly identify the required competencies (technical, interpersonal, leadership) of team members, select the right team members based on these competencies as well as their reputations, and then creating and sustaining a sense and spirit of team unity and cohesion. The team then identifies and selects the processes, methods, and tools they believe will best meet the needs of their styles, the client, and the outcomes, e.g., project deliverables, they are chartered to create. Forcing a project team to use a predefined set of tools guarantees one thing, that those tools will be used. It does not enhance the likelihood of a successful outcome. It's like giving someone a hammer and screwdriver and then telling them to

163

go figure out what they are working on and how they will make these tools work in that context.

- Value working software over comprehensive documentation. Software development teams want to do one thing, develop software that works. Working software is defined as code that does what it is supposed to, when it is supposed to, in the manner it is supposed to. Agile software development recognizes that no stack of requirements, analysis, architecture or design documentation has value if it does not enable an operational system. Development projects that are heavy on documentation are tethered to a couple of project management mindsets. The first is the "waterfall", "milestone" or "phased" approach to project management and execution. These approaches are characterized by each decision to move on to the next phase is preceded by a lengthy review. The review itself is based primarily documentation, not working deliverables. The second enabler and driver of heavy documentation is often based on a "CYA" mentality. Because projects involve the investment and commitment of substantial amounts of resources people can be very sensitive to their level of actual or perceived level of accountability. Documentation can provide an accurate accounting of how all the resources involved in a project have been engaged and utilized. Agile takes the perspective that instead of providing a large amount of documentation that shows how much work has been done in creating code, just show the actual working code.

- Customer collaboration is more important than contract negotiation. Agile development focused on IT professionals working in teams to develop software that works for customers. Sounds obvious, right? It becomes less so when you experience projects that are managed in more traditional ways. Working on "waterfall" type projects can sometimes leave people thinking the project is about developing everything but deliverables that satisfy customer needs and expectations. On non-agile projects the team can sometimes miss the mark because they adhere too much to the letter of the contract. Instead of working to be flexible to the needs of the client, the contract is used as a buffer or barrier to limit the amount of contact and engagement between people involved in the work. The reality is the contract is static. It was written and approved over a specific period of time. Upon signing it became static. Even if it does capture the complete set of requirements in a manner understandable and actionable by all the change and dynamism of the technology space and project delivery space will drive both the need and opportunity to change and evolve to maintain alignment. When Agile is applied to a software development project working software should be the first and primary measure by which a project is evaluated. Documentation should be leveraged to deliver software that works. The line between documentation being an enabler or impediment can be very fine, so it is something that requires constant attention. A key question I like to continuously ask myself is "Am I succeeding because of what I am doing or in-spite of what I am doing?" You can also ask others to answer this question about you. Sometimes the insight provided by such feedback can be powerful.

- It is more important to respond to change than it is to follow a plan. Put another way, few if any projects plans survive initial contact with the real-world completely intact. The project team then has to choose between adhering to the project plan or adjusting to the needs, requirements, and opportunities the project performance and client service delivery environment provides.

These values are implemented with the following set of principles:

- The highest priority of an Agile project is to satisfy customers through early and continuous delivery of quality products, e.g., software
- The Agile team welcomes changing requirements, even those that come late in the development process. Agile processes, tools and methods embrace and harness change for the customer's competitive advantage
- Deliverables, e.g., working software, should be delivered frequently, in time frames ranging from a couple of weeks to a couple of months, with a preference for shorter timescales
- Business people and developers should work together daily throughout the lifecycle of the project
- Assemble teams of the most talented, engaged personnel you can find, then provide them with

166

the environment and support they need and trust them to get the job done

- The most efficient and effective method of communication with and within a development team is face to face
- Deliverables that work, e.g., working software, is the primary measure of project progress
- Agile processes, methods and tools promote sustainable development. If needed, the sponsors, developers, and users should be able to maintain a constant pace indefinitely
- Simplicity, defined as the art of maximizing the amount of work not done, is essential
- The best software architectures, requirements, and designs emerge from teams that are self-organizing
- The project team reflects at regular intervals, gaining perspective and understanding on how to become even more effective, then adjusts, tunes, and aligns its behavior accordingly

Questions to Consider

1. How does your organization empower project team members to the point needed to enable them to feel both willing and able to deliver their projects in a more agile way?
2. How have changes in client needs, technology and project execution environments impacted your organizations approaches to project based client service delivery?
3. What attempts has your organization made to move to more Agile mindsets and methods?

4. What compelled the organization to embrace more Agile methods?
5. How successful were these moves to more Agile methods?
6. What enabled the moves to be successful?
7. If the attempts to move to more Agile methods were not as successful as needed or planned, what prevented them from being so?
8. Agile methods embrace practices such as communication, collaboration, velocity, small scale releases, etc. that are not new. How are these practices leveraged in your organization today?
9. What are the opportunities to improve in this regard?
10. How would improvement in this regard affect your organizations project execution and client service delivery?
11. How "close" are your project teams to the customers they support?
12. What either enables them to be close, or prevents them from it?
13. What is the impact of being close to the customer, or lack thereof, on overall project execution and client service delivery?
14. What can be done to improve in this regard?
15. How would improving in this area affect overall project execution and client service delivery?
16. Agile is known for enabling teams to approach projects based on the unique needs of the project and the clients they support. How flexible are your organizations approaches to project management and project enabled client service delivery in the context of enabling the team to

adjust or adapt to client needs, requirements, and opportunities?

17. What role do organizational values play in your organization's approach to project management, execution, and client service delivery?

18. What are the opportunities to improve in this regard?

19. How would improving in this area affect overall project performance and client service delivery?

20. How are the competencies or project team members in your organization identified?

21. How are the competencies, capabilities, and qualifications of members of your organization's project teams assured?

22. How are members of project teams selected in your organization?

23. What types of project tools does your organization provide?

24. How do project teams in your organization go about identifying, selecting and using the project tools your organization provides?

25. How are the quality, effectiveness, and usability of project management and project related client service delivery tools evaluated?

26. What is involved in determining when project management tools, processes, and resources need to be reviewed, changed, upgraded, replaced, or discarded?

27. What are the opportunities for improvement in this regard?

28. How would improvement in this area affect project execution and overall client service delivery?

29. How is documentation used on the projects your organization is involved in?
30. What are the opportunities to improve how documentation is used in support of projects your organization is involved in?
31. How would improvement in this area affect overall project execution and client service delivery?
32. Projects are defined as short term endeavors designed to produce specific deliverables that are valuable to the client. How do the project management and project enabled client service delivery methods used by your organization enable or inhibit attainment of this goal?
33. What are the opportunities to improve in this regard?
34. What must occur in order for these opportunities to become a reality?
35. How would improvement in these areas affect overall project execution and client service delivery?
36. How receptive and responsive is your organization to opportunities for improvement to your current project management methods, tools and approaches?
37. What types of legacy mindsets exist in your organization in the context of project management and the client service delivery needs and opportunities they exist to support?
38. What role does the customer play in projects your organization is currently involved in?
39. How was this role determined, decided on, or settled upon?

40. How would improvement in the area of bringing clarity to the customer role affect overall project execution and client service delivery?
41. What would have to occur in order for the changes needed to drive improvement in this area?
42. What role does the contract, statement of work, project plan and other documentation play in project planning, management, execution, and evaluation?
43. What are the opportunities to improve in this regard?
44. What would have to occur in order for these opportunities to become reality?
45. How would improvement in this area enhance overall project execution and client service delivery?
46. How is the success of projects executed your organization measured and evaluated?
47. Why is success measured and evaluated in this specific way?
48. What are the opportunities to improve in this regard?
49. What would have to occur in the organization in order for these opportunities to become reality?
50. How would improvement in this regard enhance overall project execution and client service delivery?
51. What practices, tools, methods, and technology does your organization leverage to maintain customer focus in support of project execution?
52. How is the effectiveness of these efforts measured and evaluated?

53. What are the opportunities to improve in the area of project focus on the customer?
54. What would have to occur in order for these opportunities to become reality?
55. How would improvement in this area affect overall project execution and client service delivery?
56. How responsive are your organizations project management methods, approaches, tools, processes and techniques to changes in customer requirements?
57. How is this responsiveness measured and evaluated?
58. What are the opportunities to improve in the context of change readiness and responsiveness to client service delivery needs?
59. What would have to happen in order for these opportunities to become reality?
60. How would improvement in this area enhance overall project performance and client service delivery?
61. How do projects teams in your organization currently leverage the tools, methods, and other project related and aligned resources (for guidance, to exercise control, etc.)?
62. Does the manner in which these tools are used to enhance or inhibit the ultimate delivery to the customer?
63. What are the opportunities to improve in this regard?
64. What would have to happen in order for these opportunities to become reality?

65. How would improving in this area enhance project execution and overall client service delivery?
66. What is the current mindset of your organization about project management and the role it plays in enabling and supporting client service delivery requirements?
67. What type of impact (positive / neutral / negative) does this mindset have on the current state of overall project execution and client service delivery?
68. What are the opportunities for improvement in this regard?
69. What would have to happen in order for these opportunities to become reality?
70. How would improvement in this area affect overall project execution and client service delivery?
71. How does your organization currently create and sustain the engagement of project teams and their members at a level that consistently supports the required high level of client service delivery?
72. What are the opportunities for improvement in this regard?
73. What would have to occur in order for these opportunities to become reality?
74. How would improvement in this regard affect overall project execution and client service delivery?
75. What are the current means, mediums, and modes of communication on and among projects your organization is currently involved in?
76. Why these specific means, mediums and modes?

77. How is their effectiveness currently measured and evaluated?
78. What are the opportunities to improve in this regard?
79. What would have to happen in order for these opportunities to become reality?
80. How would improvement in this area affect overall project execution and client service delivery?

Agile Characteristics

Characteristics of an Agile Project

Project management as both a philosophy and set of practices has been around as long as people have had the desire to achieve things that require systematic effort, the effort or others, or both.

Based on the previous discussion you may be getting the idea that I believe Agile is the solution to all project management needs and opportunities. Not so. There are a number of different project management methods available today. The total includes things like PMI, PRINCE2, CPM, PERT, etc. Each of these approaches has their own specific applications, e.g., environments where they work quite effectively. This is based on the fact that each approach bears specific characteristics that when properly matched with the needs of the client, situation, problem and / or opportunity enable and support a successful outcome. Such is the case with Agile as well.

Like the other project management approaches, Agile works best in very specific environments where specific characteristics are present. Such characteristics can be viewed from these perspectives:

- From the perspective of the development team Agile:

- It involves regular, frequent, and focused collaboration
- Has team members co-located with one and other as well as the customer
- Consists of no more than 50 people
- Embraces continuous learning

- From the perspective of Project Management Agile seeks to create, sustain and leverage:

  - A responsive management culture
  - Monitoring team participation
  - Continuous planning
  - Several mechanisms for providing and obtaining feedback

- From a customer perspective Agile project management addresses customer needs by:

  - Enabling involvement throughout the project
  - Making the customer easily accessible

- From a process and tool perspective Agile:

  - Creates an environment where team input is the last word on issues that are being considered and addressed
  - There are just enough tools and just enough processes to do what needs to be done
  - Allows the methods, processes and tools to be changed as needed to best suit the goal, clients and team

- From a contract perspective Agile creates:

  - Flexibility around dates and requirements
  - Cost is predicated on time and materials

Questions to Consider

1. What factors does your organization consider when determining which type of project management processes to apply to a specific project need or opportunity?
2. How are these factors identified?
3. How are the methods used to identify the factors used in project management methodology selection measured and evaluated?
4. How is this evaluation data and information used to improve the methods associated with and in support of factor identification and selection?
5. What are the opportunities to improve in this regard?
6. How would improvement in the area of factor identification and selection improve overall project management, execution and client service delivery?
7. How responsive are the current project management methods currently used by your organization to the needs of the project team?
8. What methods, tools and processes are used to evaluate the effectiveness of these tools, methods and processes.
9. How is the data and information currently collected and analyzed.
10. How is what is learned from this analysis used to improve the responsiveness of the project management delivery processes, tools, and methods?
11. What are the opportunities to improve in the area of project management responsiveness to the needs of project team members?

12. What would have to occur in order to make these opportunities a reality?
13. How responsive are the project management methods leveraged by your organization to both current state and evolving customer needs.
14. What methods, tools and processes are used to measure and evaluate the performance of project management related, enabling and supporting efforts.
15. How is this information and data analyzed?
16. How is what is learned from this analysis used to improve the responsiveness of project management methods to client needs.
17. What are the opportunities for improvement in terms of making your organizations project management methods more responsive to client needs?
18. What would have to occur in order for these opportunities to become reality?
19. How would improvement in this area affect overall project execution and client service delivery.
20. How are specific tools, methods, and processes selected for use on projects your organization is involved with?
21. What types of tools, methods, and processes are used on and in support of projects your organization is involved with?
22. How is the effectiveness of these tools, methods, and processes evaluated?
23. What are the opportunities to improve in the area of selecting tools, processes and methods in supporting of projects your organization is involved in?

24. What are the opportunities to improve in this regard?
25. What would have to happen in order for these opportunities to become reality?
26. How would improvement in this area enhance overall project execution and client service delivery?

The Agile Methodologies

The Agile Methodologies

This portion of the discussion focused on the Agile methodologies. To begin, let's identify the themes all Agile methodologies have in common:

- Agile development teams focus on developing and completing features in the applications they are working on vs. simply checking off on tasks and activities listed on the project plan
- Agile teams work in the context of change, responding to it and even attempting to anticipate it rather than preventing it, blocking it or denying it
- Documentation is secondary to working software
- Time boxing, the practice of identifying specific periods of time and the specific work that will be accomplished within them, is not designed to make people work harder. Instead it helps to ensure tough decisions are not deferred and that the most important bits of work are prioritized appropriately
- Planning and estimation are team activities and should not be performed by a lone project manager
- Feedback collected near the end of the project arrives too late to be of any use to the project. Feedback should be elicited regularly. This enables the team to make any needed adjustments during the project, when they can make the desired or required difference. Short iterations driving frequent delivery to customers provide an excellent mechanism for meaningful, sustainable feedback loops

- Projects must be able to adjust their direction as a result of internal feedback and external events
- Agile development is not about identifying and reusing tools and techniques that are believed to be universally applicable and to work in every situation. It is about creating and sustaining a project performance and client service delivery environment as well as an organizational culture that allows skilled professionals to readily adapt to changing requirements and situations
- While process is a necessary component of software development, an over specified project actually slows down development
- No amount of process can replace engaged and talented people

Extreme Programming (XP)

XP is perhaps the best and most widely known of the Agile methodologies. It is also the only method that focuses primarily on the programming side of software development.

Any project management and software development methodology that provides a team with the ability to achieve its goals more effectively and efficiently is bound to be embraced by others. Such is the case with XP. Other Agile and even non-agile project teams leverage many of the practices, procedures, and tasks.

XP is heavily programmer centric. On a team leveraging XP even team members who are primarily responsible for non-programming tasks are capable of, enabled and empowered to performing programming work. This is a key strength of XP. In addition, by making

186

programmers responsible for their own analysis and management XP also cuts many of the levels and barriers associated with more traditional development methodologies.

XP is also unique among Agile methodologies because of its laser like focus on testing. XP is the only Agile methodology to prescribe how testing should be integrated into the software development process. The reality is XP cannot be implemented without testing. In addition, many Agile practices inspired by XP, such as continuous integration, simple design and refactoring, cannot be implemented without testing.

XP is based on the values of communication, simplicity, feedback and courage. As values, they are intended to guide the thinking, decisions and actions of the XP team. To help team members clarify and implement the values, XP embraces specific practices:

1. Test driven development – the practice and discipline of writing tests prior top writing code. Tests are an invaluable way of capturing requirements and ensuring the code that is designed and delivered ultimately meets requirements.
2. Planning game – a set of rules and moves that can be used to simplify the release planning process.
3. Whole team – the programming team, management, the customer and all other pertinent parties work within the same open workspace to get the project done.
4. Pair programming – two programmers working at one workstation can actually produce higher

quality code without costing extra time over the lifecycle of the project. This is due in large part that the longer amount of personnel time accounted for in coding is more than made up for by reduced amount of time spent fixing problems and correcting errors.

5. Design improvement – the team needs to keep the code clean by regularly taking the opportunity to clean up complex code or simplify sections that are confusing.

6. Small releases – small releases are the cornerstone of iterative development and time boxing. Small releases increase the frequency of delivery of working software to the customers. It also provides greater flexibility in making needed changes. Time boxing clarifies expectations by specifying the amount of time to be spent completing a working piece of code to the customer.

7. Simple design – XP focuses on satisfying known client needs with code that performs as needed now, not what they think they might need in the future. Change is a constant in XP world. Short iterations enable the team to be as flexible as it can and needs to be in terms of adapting to change. But, trying to predict what might happen in the future and then trying to design a solution for that possibility today is like chasing shadows.

8. Coding standards – a coding standard is one that is known, understood, accepted, and used by the entire development team.

9. Sustainable pace – teams that work too hard burn out. Projects with burned out teams fail. Sustainable pace focuses on keeping team

members working when they are in good shape and letting them stop when they are tired. This practice was once known as the 40 hour work week. In addition, keeping in mind that software development is as much art as it is science, that it involves creativity as much as the ability to think pragmatically and logically. There will be times where programmers are "in the zone" and will put in very long hours and accomplish a great deal. There may be other times where they are stuck on a problem and the best thing they can do is walk away from it for a bit.

XP is highly iterative. It is characterized by a steady rhythm of iterations lasting from one to four weeks. The only three things an XP needs to create its first iteration is an iteration worth of user stories, a decision on which technology will be used to satisfy the requirements specified in the user stories, and funding. It is this compact set of requirements that allows XP to be highly effective in rapid prototyping.

An iteration is complete when the team delivers a fully programmed, fully tested, production ready version of the system that meets client needs and expectations. In XP, every one to four week iteration can be viewed as a release.

The reality is that this frequency of release can be disruptive for a business. In order for a software iteration or release to be useful the client must be able to put it to work. All of the parts of the system and organization that will be using and be impacted by the use of the application need to be ready. If this is not the case then frequent XP iterations can actually be disruptive to the point of being damaging. To lessen the disruption the XP team can bundle a group of iterations into a single release. Bundling and scheduling of releases can then be aligned with a schedule that best works for the client.

Now as you read through this you may be thinking "that sounds a whole lot like waterfall project management". However, I caution you not to make this assumption. As an Agile approach to software development, XP has the customer working directly with the development team every step of the way. The development team still creates and delivers iterations based on small time boxes of work. The small iterations resulting deliverables are still designed specifically to meet known customer needs based on the user stories and client input. The fact that Agile in general and XP specifically enables the deliverable schedule to be flexed in response to client readiness and needs is perhaps the greatest difference between XP and waterfall based approaches.

SCRUM

SCRUM is based on the values of commitment, focus, openness, respect, and courage. While XP is primarily focused on the programmers, SCRUM is a management focused Agile methodology. It can be implemented in a wide variety of project driven environments. This methodology provides the guidance needed to direct a project in an environment of high changeability and where different parties within the customer environment have conflicting or competing interests. In comparison to XP, SCRUM is lighter on the programming side. While SCRUM does stipulate the team deliver software that works and has been tested is does not prescribe how the project team should go about doing this.

190

The SCRUM methodology is based on the concept of empirical process control. Contrast this with the concept of defined process control, where the production process for a product or deliverable is initially defined and continually refined to meet an acceptable level of cost and quality. Empirical process control aligns with the likelihood of the unpredictability and associated complexity of software development projects (including requirements, goals, technologies and the general business climate). Attempts to use defined process control do not provide the flexibility and adaptability needed to effect adjust to dynamic situations and changing client needs and requirements. This is where SCRUM is effective. By using empirical process control teams leveraging SCRUM methodologies control cost and quality by:

- Making the aspects of the development process that most affect project outcomes visible and transparent to customers
- Allow customers to inspect the product regularly and ensure little variation from stated objectives
- If an inspection shows a variation beyond acceptable limits the customer is positioned to quickly adapt the development process, resulting product, or both

SCRUM makes a clear distinction between the team whose responsibility it is to deliver the project (programmers, testers, analysts and technical writers) and everyone else (stakeholders, business users, and upper management). Personnel in the latter group select the features the system will possess and the attributes it will exhibit as well as providing regular input to the work the development team is doing. The programmers perform the day-to-day management required to build the system. Even more than XP, SCRUM puts the project teams success or failure in its own hands. In SCRUM the customer has a clear and daily view into the activity of the team. The customer is also expected to exert control on the project at the beginning of each 30 day sprint (also known as an iteration in XP as well as time box from a general Agile perspective). However, in the SCRUM approach the customer is not allowed to interfere with the teams' activity or work during the sprint. Once the sprint is completed the customer has the opportunity to address any issues that have arisen during the sprint prior to the beginning of the next sprint.

A SCRUM master leads a SCRUM project. This person can be the team lead of project manager. However, specific competencies are required in order to be successful in this role. The SCRUM master bridges the gap between the project team and the customer. One of their primary roles is to ensure all parties are adhering to and leveraging the values, roles, principles and practices that comprise SCRUM. Enabling competencies in this area include communication, negotiation, problem solving, and conflict management, as well as the requisite technical skills.

SCRUM recognizes there may be several people related to and involved with a project (stakeholders, customers, etc.). Each of the groups and the individuals that comprise them will bring their own interests, concerns, worries and needs to the project space. However, it is important to keep in mind that a single person, the Product Owner, is solely responsible for bringing the concerns and needs to the development team. The Product Owner is also responsible for specifying and communicating to the development team what they need to be working and developing at the start of each sprint. The Product Owner is responsible for negotiating the requirements and needs among the various stakeholders and interested parties. The Product Owner then prioritizes these needs on the Product Backlog. The Product Backlog contains an ever evolving list of functional and technical features for the system being developed. In order for SCRUM to work the Product Owner must be single individual, not a group or committee. This single point of contact for all project related needs, features, attributes, etc. helps to ensure the development team is not constantly being hit with countless requirements from a limitless number of stakeholders and other interested or impacted parties.

Time boxing is another important feature of the 30 day sprint. A big complaint (and opportunity for improvement) on projects is the fact that many of them go past scheduled deadlines or deliverable dates. The causes for this include unclear, vague, or ambiguous expectations, changing requirements, etc. Given that each sprint lasts 30 days time boxing forces the Product Owner to make the tough decisions about functionality and design, specifically what needs to be included in a release and what can or should be left to another sprint, or left out completely. This allows the development team to stay out of low productivity activities by requiring customers to discuss amongst themselves what the application needs to do in order to satisfy requirements. This level sets expectations in terms of what the development team will and will not work on during the 30 day sprint.

Another feature of the SCRUM approach is found in the use of daily SCRUM meetings. These meetings facilitate daily communication between the development team and stakeholders. The SCRUMs ensure the team communicates frequently, that no one on the team wanders off course, and that the Product Owner and customers are made aware of problems and roadblocks as well as overall status on a regular basis.

Each SCRUM sprint concludes with the delivery of a product increment (deliverable) that demonstrably positively impacts and furthers the progress of the project. This increment should be a production ready release, a substantial step forward in functionality, or the proofing of a risky component. While SCRUM sprint goals provide clarity and focus, it is important to understand they are not written in stone. The process needs to work for the team and customers as much as the team and customers are beholden to the process. Towards this end, the goals may be adjusted based on agreement between the team and product owner.

Of all the Agile methodologies SCRUM is the one that can be established without customization in the largest and most varied number of environments. This stems from its overall light weight, non-intrusive management processes and a notable lack of distinct management policies and procedures. This light touch means SCRUM techniques and tools can be used to wrapper existing programming practices without making significant changes to the way the team does it daily work. However, to achieve this state SCRUM requires the customer not meddle with the time while it is in sprint mode and that the team may alter sprint goals as required based on the ease or difficulty of the task at hand. These changes of course are done with the agreement of the Product Owner.

Feature Driven Development (FDD)

FDD tackles both the management and programming activity. It is able to do this in a scalable way, having been used on projects with as many as 250 people and lasting as long as 18 months. In order to scale to this level effectively FDD requires a system wide modeling activity that us performed at the beginning of the project. This work, combined with an initial flexible development and execution plan has led some to say FDD is not really Agile. However, FDD is highly iterative, requires and relies upon low level analysis and design activities in the same iteration as it completes functionality, and engages its customers through the entire lifecycle of the project. As such it is tuned to enable the project team to recognize and respond to change.

The key elements of an FDD project are:

- Develop an Overall Model
- Build a Features List
- Plan by Feature
- Design by Feature
- Build by Feature

The FDD project takes shape when architecture is front loaded and planning is initiated. The first three processes, Develop an Overall Model, Build a Feature List, and Plan by Feature are performed only once in their entirety. However, the project can return to these activities if there are significant changes to the amount of or timing of the work.

In the first process, Develop an Overall Model, the team works with the customer to produce an overall model of the system. The model is meant only to be completed to the shapes that will make the system. It is intended to force individual ideas and assumptions out into the open at the beginning of a project. This allows misunderstandings to be resolved early. It also helps to ensure the team has a complete, collective understanding of the system.

In the second process, Build a Features List, the project management team uses the overall model to produce a features list. The system is broken down into features (defined as bits of functionality that are useful to the customer) and is grouped into feature sets. The feature sets are prioritized and a minimally complete system is identified (representing the minimum number of features required for the system to be valuable to the customer).

The third FDD process, Plan by Feature, provides for the development of a feature schedule characterized by feature sets. Each feature set is planned for completion in a specific month (FDD does not provide exact dates). Chief programmers then divide up the feature sets. Programmers are assigned to code the specific classes identified and specified in the model.

The completion of each feature set occurs over one or more iterations Plan by Feature and Design by Feature activities. Each Chief Programmer works through their list of feature sets, creating a new feature team for each feature set. Feature sets are then refined with the assistance of Domain Experts, designed as a part of group activity, built and unit tested, reviewed by the Feature Team and then integrated into the system.

FDD lends itself to a need that is more structured and design forward then is found in other Agile methodologies, while still enabling a streamlined management process. These management processes are founded on Agile values and practices such as short iterations, customer involvement, and testing.

A successful implementation of FDD is founded upon a specific set of best practices. As with XP's best practices teams may gain some benefit by adopting one or more of them. However, it is important to keep in mind that some of the practices are built to reinforce one and other. In these cases the full power and benefit of the practices can only be achieved when they are all in action.

- Domain Object Modeling – the domain model is an overall roadmap of the system to be built. It consists of a set of high level diagrams that depict the relationships between classes of objects and sequence diagrams that illustrate and demonstrate the behavior of the total system as well as its respective components.
- Develop By Feature – this is a practice common to all Agile methodologies as well as being a cornerstone of Agile development.
- Class Ownership – the code class is an encapsulation mechanism that is common among object oriented programming languages. Class ownership is the enactment of code ownership where each class within the system is assigned to a specific programmer. This is the opposite of XP's collective ownership approach, where everyone on the team owns everything the team is developing.

- Feature Teams – this practice is founded on the strict application of class ownership. The method is employed by class owners to complete features that span multiple classes. Since features commonly involve more than one class feature teams are the common approach to design and development in FDD.
- Inspections – inspections that focus on the identification of defects and do not intimidate or humiliate the programmers can significantly increase the quality of the system under development. Secondary benefits to inspections include improved transfer of knowledge and greater conformance to coding and design standards.
- Regular Build Schedule – teams need to build the complete system according to regular intervals to identify integration errors early. This also enables an up to date system to always be available to the client. The build may be performed hourly, daily, or even weekly depending on the size of the project and the amount of time it takes to perform a complete system compile and integration. This practice is similar to the automated build practice.
- Reporting / Visibility of Results – regular and easy to understand status updates are needed to guide a project. They also help keep customers and stakeholders aware of the project's status so they can plan and act accordingly.

There are also six key roles on an FDD project. They are:

- Project manager

- Chief architect
- Development manager
- Chief programmers
- Class owners
- Domain experts

Test Driven Development

Test-driven development (TDD) is a software development process that relies on the repetition of a very short development cycle: first the developer writes a failing automated test that defines a desired improvement or new function, then produces code to pass that test and finally refactors the new code to work perform as required by the test. The tests are based on specific customer requirements as defined and described by user stories and use cases.

Test-driven development requires developers to create automated unit tests that define code requirements (immediately) before writing the code itself. The tests contain assertions that are either true or false. Passing the tests confirms correct behavior as developers evolve and refactor the code. Developers often use testing frameworks to create and automatically run sets of test cases.

In test-driven development, each new feature begins with writing a test. This test must inevitably fail because it is written before the feature has been implemented. (If it does not fail, then either the proposed "new" feature already exists or the test is defective.) To write a test, the developer must clearly understand the feature's specification and requirements. The developer can accomplish this through use cases and user stories that cover the requirements and exception conditions. This could also imply a variant, or

199

modification of an existing test. This is a differentiating feature of test-driven development versus writing unit tests after the code is written: it makes the developer focus on the requirements before writing the code, a subtle but important difference.

Next the team runs all of the tests, paying specific attention to which ones fail. This validates that the test harness is working correctly and that the new test does not mistakenly pass without requiring any new code. This step also tests the test itself, in the negative: it rules out the possibility that the new test will always pass, and therefore be worthless. The new test should also fail for the expected reason. This increases confidence (although it does not entirely guarantee) that it is testing the right thing, and will pass only in intended cases.

The next step is to write some code that will cause the test to pass. The new code written at this stage will not be perfect and may, for example, pass the test in an inelegant way. That is acceptable because later steps will improve and hone it.

It is important that the code written is *only* designed to pass the test; no further (and therefore untested) functionality should be predicted and 'allowed for' at any stage.

If all test cases now pass, the programmer can be confident that the code meets all the tested requirements. This is a good point from which to begin the final step of the cycle.

Now the code can be cleaned up as necessary. By re-running the test cases, the developer can be confident that code refactoring is not damaging any existing functionality. The concept of removing duplication is an important aspect of any software design. In this case, however, it also applies to removing any duplication between the test code and the production code.

Starting with another new test, the cycle is then repeated to push forward the functionality. The size of the steps should always be small, with as few as 1 to 10 edits between each test run. If new code does not rapidly satisfy a new test, or other tests fail unexpectedly, the programmer should undo or revert in preference to excessive debugging Continuous integration helps by providing revertible checkpoints. When using external libraries it is important not to make increments that are so small as to be effectively merely testing the library itself, unless there is some reason to believe that the library is buggy or is not sufficiently feature-complete to serve all the needs of the main program being written.

The Crystal Methodologies

Crystal is based on the idea that different projects need different sorts of methodologies. The Crystal family is a set of methodologies that share the same set of principles and building blocks. Each methodology within the family targets a different type of project execution and client service delivery situation or set of circumstances. The Crystal approach embraces the variations that exist in this environment and addresses it with a catalogue of sample methodologies. This cataloguing is based on project size and criticality. Criticality is measured by the amount of rigor required from the methodology. The higher the risk associated with the activity of a function or feature the higher the criticality.

Other important Crystal attributes include the recognition that as a project gets larger a method and approach heavier on process and control is required. Crystal is also explicit in that it will willingly trade efficiency (cost savings and time) for an increased chance off success.

Once the characteristics and opportunities of the project are known a base methodology can be selected from the Crystal family. It can then be tailored then to the needs and opportunities of its particular environment and circumstances.

Key characteristics of catalogued Crystal methodologies include being:

- People focused
- Communication centric
- Highly tolerant

Crystal Clear

Crystal Clear is designed and intended for a project consisting of up to eight people working one team working in the same area. Crystal Clear, like all Crystal methodologies, is focused on eliciting feedback, reflection, and tuning. After the team comes together and begins their work, feedback, reflection, and tuning. After the team comes together and begins their work feedback is a key input into continually fine tuning the development and client service delivery work and supporting processes.

Crystal Clear projects must complete at least two delivery cycles and release functionality at least twice during the project. This allows it to gain real feedback from the customer in the middle of the project while there is still time to adjust.

To achieve the required level of performance a project leveraging Crystal Clear will have three key roles. They are:

- Executive Sponsor
- Lead Designer
- Ambassador User

In keeping with the spirit and intent of the Crystal catalogue of methodologies, Crystal Clear may serve as a stepping stone to another Agile method for a team. Teams using Crystal Clear are provided much greater freedom in identifying which Agile practices they will use. This enables learning and the gain in confidence associated with successfully using a new approach. For example, a team just beginning to venture into Agile may want to test the waters with Crystal Clear, and then once confident the can leverage the method to deliver effectively they could decide to move to XP or another Agile methodology that would enable them to deliver and execute even more effectively.

Crystal Orange

Crystal Orange was designed for projects where both cost and time to market are important, that involve 25 – 50 people, and have a duration from 1 – 2 years. It can be used for projects where discretionary money is at risk and may be extended to projects associated with essential money by adding additional verification and testing activities. Crystal Orange leverages multiple roles, focuses on the creation and makeup of sub-teams and places additional emphasis on documentation (including requirements and user interface documentation).

Summary of the Crystal Perspective

The "every project is unique" mindset built into Crystal methodologies makes them amenable to a wide variety of personnel and software development environments and requirements. The Crystal methodologies are highly configurable in that they allow ready situations with other equivalent policies and processes.

The Crystal approaches can also be useful in an organization that is attempting to execute many diverse projects. The Crystal Methodologies can help rationalize a portfolio of projects of projects by providing a set of base methodologies that provide just enough process across the organization.

Adaptive Software Development (ASD)

ASD is focused at the project management level and its relationship with the organization it serves. It has some of the characteristics of traditional project management including formal initiation and review procedures. Unlike XP and SCRUM., ASD folds the planning of future iterations into an initial stage of the project. Like other Agile methodologies ASD argues that command and control is a liability in environments characterized by high change because it slows the sharing of information and impedes quick, accurate, informed decisions. The project manager in the ASD environment enables a collaborative environment, helps to identify project goals, removes obstacles and creates and sustains an environment where things are able to happen.

An ASD project is mission focused, feature based, iterative, time based, risk driven and change tolerant.

The Adaptive Lifecycle

An ASD project flow is characterized by three phases, those being:

- Speculate
- Collaborate
- Learn

An ASD project typically cycles through all three phases every three to four weeks. The Speculate and Learn phases also bookend the process.

The open access to information based on continuous collaboration combined with the iterative nature of ASD are meant to enable and sustain an environment in which project leaders collaborate with the organization as the iterations are completed to adapt the direction of the project toward the most desirable outcome.

Speculation

ASD replaces project planning with speculation. This phase is designed to help the project and its organization appreciate the uncertainty behind the system they are about to build. Speculation simply means that planning has an element of uncertainty built into it. This awareness enhances flexibility. This element is also unlike other Agile methods in that it includes specific documentation recommendations.

205

These simple and straight-forward documents serve as a guide and are refined throughout the project life-cycle.

There are five steps in the speculation phase of ASD. The first step involves gathering information, including mission, objectives, and initial size and scope estimates and by project risks. Second, the entire project length is determined. Third, the number and length of iterations is determined. Fourth, the objective for each iteration is identified. Fifth, features are assigned to each iteration.

Collaborate

This is where programming activity occurs. Each cycle must deliver something useful to the customer. However, there is no requirement that the deliverables coming out of the iterations are production worthy. Like SCRUM, ASD does not state how programmers should go about performing technical activities.

Instead of focusing on design, build and test activities ASD calls for the project manager to focus on installing a collaborative outline across the entire project team. Collaboration is a catalyst in creating and sustaining self-organizing, high performing teams. However, there is no single or sure method for fostering collaboration. It is founded on trust. Anything that will further and enhance trust is value adding.

Learn

ASD highlights the importance of feedback from and among people more than the average Agile methodology. For example, each iteration within ASD ends with a quality

206

review. During the quality review the project team solicits and considers all input from the customers. This is Priority 1. Other input is solicited from and provided by the members of the programming teams. In addition, the quality of the features as well as the overall status of the project is reviewed.

To enable and sustain an effective learning environment ASD recommends three processes, those being focus groups with customers, technical reviews of software, and a project wide post-mortem.

Dynamic Systems Development Method (DSDM)

DSDM endorses many of the practices associated with the other Agile methodologies previously discussed. As such, DSDM calls for a collaborative relationship between project team and customer, the use of time boxing to control scope as well as focus on business value and focus on testing to ensure the quality, reliability and maintainability of the systems that are developed.

The Nine Principles of DSDM

DSDM focuses on building systems in short amounts of time, in small increments, with participation from end users, customers, and developers. All parties enter the process with the mindset that tradeoffs need to be made among features with more and less value. DSM leverages nine principles to achieve this goal.

- Active user involvement is critical
- The team must be empowered to make decisions

- The focus is on frequent delivery of products that matter most to customers
- Fitness for business purpose is the essential criterion for acceptance of a deliverable
- Iterative and incremental development is necessary to converge on an accurate business solution
- All changes made during development are reversible
- Requirements are base lined at a high level
- Testing is integrated throughout the lifecycle
- Collaboration and cooperation among all stakeholders is essential

DSDM views a failure it adhere to one or more of the nine principles, without the use of appropriate mitigation strategies, as an act that introduces significant right into the project.

DSDM also leverages phases, seven in all. They are:

- Feasibility and business study
- Identify functional prototype, agree to schedule, create prototype, review
- Functional model iteration
- Identify design prototype, agree on schedule, create prototype, review
- Design and build iteration
- User approval, train users, implement business review
- Implement iteration

How a DSDM works through the phases is left to the designs and needs of the project team and client base being served.

DSDM schedules work within time boxes of two to six weeks. DSDM uses this time boxing approach to ensure tough decisions regarding functionality and technical requirements are made and to enable regular, rapid and accurate feedback.

DSDM also has a significant downside. In order to use it an organization must pay to become a member of the DSDM consortium. However, this does provide the benefit of being able to influence the evolution of the methodology. While this may deter some smaller organizations from using it, its reliance on short iterations, testing, modeling, prototyping makes it effective in a number of different and varied project environments. DSDM may deliver just the right amount of Agile to be effective.

Lean Software Development

Lean Software Development defines the maturity of an organization by how quickly and reliably it can serve its customers. Process documentation and even best practices all take a back seat to the overall goal of operational excellence.

Lean Software Development is not a methodology in the same sense as the others methods we have discussed. It does not propose or lay out a specific set of processes to be followed. Instead, Lean provides a toolkit of ideas and principles that guide the effort but are not concrete instructions on what to and what not to do. This enables the team to adjust its approach based on the specific client needs and opportunities.

Lean Thinking

Lean Software Development is based on the theory and principles of lean production, a process pioneered by Toyota. Specifically Toyota focused on eliminating waste in both the process and parts being used in the manufacturing system. This enables a dramatic reduction in the cycle time required to deliver to the client once an order has been received. Ant resources that are sitting idle are seen as waste. In the same context, decisions made earlier than actually needed in the software development process make a commitment to a specific direction that are difficult and expensive to undo. As such, these types of decisions create waste.

Lean development takes lean manufacturing principles and applies them to software development. In that context those principles are:

- Eliminate waste – waste is defined as any activity, artifact or output that does not add value to the system or to the work being done or that needs to be done. This includes unnecessary documentation, components built only to end up not being used. Waste can be thought of as anything that slows down the project team from giving the customer that they need and expect.
- Amplify learning – while the production process is focused on reducing variation the development process is focused on defining the right product or system. Project teams need to be constantly

working to put systems in place and work to continually amplify learning.

- Decide as late as possible – this principle recognizes the fact that change is a continuous force. The later the design and development decisions can and are made the greater the likelihood the deliverables will match the customer requirements. This idea of basically keeping your options open allows the design team to capitalize on changes that are known to be happening as well as those that cannot even be predicted until they occur.
- Deliver as fast as possible – delivering working software quickly and as needed instead of waiting to deliver everything at once helps reinforce the previous three principles. By focusing on delivering what is needed now the team is able to hold off decisions about what might be needed later. Learning is amplified because earlier deliveries enable the customer to better understand and provide feedback on the portions of the system that have yet to be developed. Reducing the time between a request for functionality and the delivery of that functionality also reduces waste.
- Empower the team – decisions cannot be put until as late as possible if they need to be made by managers or other high level people in the organization. When developers are provided with appropriate guidance and engaged in activities related to design and process they make better decisions on their own than anyone could make for them.

- Build on integrity – integrity means the product or system is put together well, operates smoothly as well as how it was designed and intended to operate, and is easy to maintain. Integrity is founded in good leadership, domain knowledge, communication and discipline, not simply good practice and process.
- See the whole – complex systems require expertise that is both broad and deep. A common pitfall in product development is the tendency to over emphasize ones expertise in a given area to the detriment of the entire system. A lopsided approach can be taken at the individual, project and even organizational level because in each case the entity will want to maximize performance in its own area of specialization. The integrity of the system is based on how well the parts fit and work together, not simply the quality of each individual part.

Questions to Consider

1. In the context of your organizations current approach to project execution and client service delivery what is the focus of the specific processes, tools, and methods as well as the overall project management philosophy?
2. How is the effectiveness of these various applications measured and evaluated?
3. What are the opportunities for improvement?
4. What would have to occur in order for these opportunities to become reality?

5. How would improvement in this area enhance overall project execution and client service delivery?

6. What type of client service delivery environment are projects in your organization executed and delivered in? Specifically is it one that is static, where the client needs and expectations are known at the beginning and remain consistent throughout? Is it one where client needs and service delivery opportunities are initially ambiguous but become clearer as the work moves forward? Is the client service delivery environment characterized by continuous change?

7. How does the environment the project is executed in affect the selection and execution of your organizations approach to the project?

8. How is the selection and application of the project management method measured and evaluated in the context of the impact it has on project execution and client service delivery?

9. What are the opportunities for improvement in this regard?

10. What would have to happen in order for these opportunities to become reality?

11. How would improvement in this area enhance project execution and overall client service delivery?

12. How responsive are your organizations approaches to project management and execution to change?

13. How is the impact of this responsiveness or lack thereof on project execution and client service delivery measured and evaluated?

14. What are the opportunities for improvement in this regard?
15. What would have to happen in order for those opportunities to become reality?
16. How would improvement in this area affect overall project execution and client service delivery?
17. How responsive is organizational management to requests from the project team to apply a different approach to a current project based on the needs of the client and the opportunities presented by the situation?
18. How is the value and impact of management control and oversight in this area measured and evaluated?
19. What are the opportunities for improvement in this regard?
20. What would have to happen in order for these opportunities to become reality?
21. How would improvement in this area affect overall project execution and client service delivery?
22. What is defined as a deliverable in the context of your organizations current project execution and client service delivery methods?
23. How is the impact of this definition of a project deliverable on project execution and client service delivery evaluated?
24. What are the opportunities for improvement in this regard?
25. What would have to happen in order for these opportunities to become reality?

26. How would improvement in this area enhance overall project execution and client service delivery?
27. What role does organizational management currently play in the success or failure of projects your organization is currently involved in?
28. How is the value of this activity measured and evaluated?
29. What are the opportunities for improvement in this regard?
30. What would have to happen in order for these opportunities to become reality?
31. How would improvement in this area enhance overall project execution and client service delivery?
32. What role does the project management and client service delivery schedule play in projects your organization is involved in?
33. How is the effectiveness and impact of current project-related schedule management measured and evaluated in the context of its impact on project execution and client service delivery?
34. What are the opportunities for improvement in this regard?
35. What would have to happen in order for these opportunities to become reality?
36. How would improvement in this area enhance overall project execution and client service delivery?
37. How is the effectiveness of these practices and their impact on overall project execution and client service delivery measured and evaluated?
38. What are the opportunities for improvement in this regard?

39. How would improvement in this area affect overall project execution and client service delivery?
40. How are users brought into the project management processes your organization currently uses?
41. How is the effectiveness of these practices and their impact on overall project execution and client service delivery measured and evaluated?
42. What are the opportunities for improvement in this regard?
43. How would improvement in this area affect overall project execution and client service delivery?
44. How are project teams empowered to make decisions on the projects they are involved in?
45. How is the effectiveness of these practices and their impact on overall project execution and client service delivery measured and evaluated?
46. What are the opportunities for improvement in this regard?
47. How would improvement in this area affect overall project execution and client service delivery?
48. What role does frequent delivery of products resulting from projects play on projects your organization is currently involved in?
49. How is the effectiveness of these practices and their impact on overall project execution and client service delivery measured and evaluated?
50. What are the opportunities for improvement in this regard?

51. How would improvement in this area affect overall project execution and client service delivery?
52. How is the concept of fitness for use currently applied on projects in your organization?
53. How is the effectiveness of these practices and their impact on overall project execution and client service delivery measured and evaluated?
54. What are the opportunities for improvement in this regard?
55. How would improvement in this area affect overall project execution and client service delivery?
56. How is testing applied on projects in your organization?
57. How is the effectiveness of these practices and their impact on overall project execution and client service delivery measured and evaluated?
58. What are the opportunities for improvement in this regard?
59. How would improvement in this area affect overall project execution and client service delivery?

Agile Practices

Agile Practices

For some organizations making a move to more Agile methods can represent a dramatic shift. Regardless of how large the change is, having a plan, a structured approach to what you are seeking to achieve and methods on how it will be achieved greatly increases the likelihood of success. Like all project management and project enabled client service delivery processes, Agile bears specific practices that are proven effective at enhancing overall project performance. These include:

- Gaining genuine partnership with the customer
- Communicate and collaborate more, document less
- Get to work on code that works

Taking this approach can also lesson resistance to change. Other methods that can be used to select Agile practices include:

- Current worst problem – identify your projects or your client's worst problems, pair it with an Agile practice that best addresses it, gain buy in from relevant and impacted parties. Once the problem is solved apply it to the next worst problem.
- Biggest bang for the buck – determine which Agile practice, if implemented today, will deliver the best combination of fastest and largest return on investment (ROI). This method should be applied to something that takes limited time to implement, has the greatest likelihood for success and will have a visibly positive effect on the project.

- Easiest thing first, hardest thing second – this approach steers the team to an early victory. Doing this enhances learning and confidence.

There will also be situations where the team needs to reject a practice. When doing this it is important for the team to evaluate and understand why the practice was rejected. Key considerations include:

- Was there another Agile practice that should have been implemented before trying to implement the practice under review?
- Did everyone associated with the practice really understand it before the team attempted to implement it and do they understand it to the required level now?
- Is the project trying to "go Agile" too quickly or too slowly?
- Did the practice fail simply because there was no second or third practice to help reinforce it?
- Was there something about the project environment or technology that caused the implementation of the practice to fail?
- Should the team attempt another implementation of this practice in the future?
- Are there other practices similar to the one being dealt with that will be encountered in the future?

When transitioning to Agile it is important to adopt practices before adopting tools. What this means is that you need to understand what you are working to achieve and how you are going to achieve it before you start looking for specific things, e.g., tools. Tools can help us do things faster, more efficiently, and to a higher level of quality. But, we have to know the proper context to use those tools in. Practices help us understand context. Here is a basic method that can help you understand context:

- Start very simple
- Learn with simple, easy to understand and use tools
- Produce results
- Learn from both success and failure
- Transition to more advanced tools

For example, a key Agile practice is to program in pairs. Here is how paired programming could work in the context of the method we just discussed:

- Start with a simple programming task
- Set a specific goal the paired team will work towards
- Produce code
- Measure the performance of the programming pair against expectations
- Determine where the key learning and improvement points are
- Repeat

Questions to Consider

1. What are the known opportunities for improvement in the area of project execution and client service delivery in your organization?
2. What is being done to leverage these opportunities?

3. What organizational forces are enabling or enhancing the changes needed to bring these opportunities into reality?
4. What organizational forces are blocking progress in this area?
5. How would improvement in this area enhance overall project execution and client service delivery?
6. What needs to happen in order to make these opportunities a reality?
7. How does the current worst problem your client is facing weigh on its selection as an area of project focus as well as the tools and methods selected to address it?
8. What are the opportunities to improve in this regard?
9. What would have to happen in order for these opportunities to become a reality?
10. How would improvement in this area enhance overall project execution and client service delivery?
11. How does the current biggest opportunity your client is aware of bear on its selection as an area of project focus as well as the tools and methods selected to address it?
12. What are the opportunities to improve in this regard?
13. What would have to happen in order for these opportunities to become a reality?
14. How would improvement in this area enhance overall project execution and client service delivery?

Selecting an Approach that Fits

Selecting an Approach that Fits

While any project may benefit from adopting one or more Agile practices it is not a given that every project would benefit from transitioning to or adopting an Agile methodology.

The following variables can help when considering whether or not to leverage Agile:

- Size – Agile / 5 people, Traditional / 500 people
- Criticality – Agile / Comfortable with risk, Traditional / Not comfortable with risk
- People – Agile / Above average personnel, Traditional / At or below average personnel
- Client Environment – Agile / Change oriented and comfortable with ambiguity, Traditional / Change averse and seek out certainty

Size

While there are Agile methodologies that are in theory scalable to larger projects team size cannot be entirely discounted when considering if a project can leverage an Agile approach effectively. The larger the team the number of communication links, the larger the number of lines of communication, the more formal the means and methods of communication become, and the greater the likelihood and risk of miscommunication. The following formula bears this out. The number of possible lines on a project is calculated by taking the total number of personnel on the project, N, multiplying that by itself minus 1 (N-1), then dividing by 2 or:

$$N * (N-1) / 2$$

Let's say you have a project with 10 team members and 10 stakeholders. The total number of communication channels is 20*(19) / 2 or 190 different channels of communication. Adding another 5 team members to the project, bring the total number of personnel to 25 and you take the number of communication channels to 300. Take the total number of project team members and stakeholders to 500 and you have a total 124,750 communication channels. With each additional channel of communication you have an added level of complexity, possible miscommunication, and potential negative impact on project execution and client service delivery.

Size itself should not be considered a deal breaker until it reaches 100 (with its 4950 channels of communication). Even then it may be possible to break this large of a team down into smaller groups that enable Agile methods.

Personnel

Personnel are the cornerstones of any Agile project. The qualities, ranked in order of importance, needed most from Agile team members are:

- Ability and willingness to continually communicate and collaborate
- Technical skill
- Experience with Agile development

The willingness and ability of team members, and everyone involved with the project for that matter, is paramount. Agile operates based on the principle of responsiveness and adaptability. Both are enabled by communication and collaboration. In addition, unlike technical skills and experience with Agile, communication skills are not easily taught.

Criticality

Criticality represents the potential for loss due to defect in the system delivered. On the low end of criticality is the potential for loss of comfort. On the high end is the potential for loss of life. Agile teams are routinely assigned to project-related errors could result in loss of comfort as well as money, either discretionary or essential.

As criticality increases projects typically apply more upfront planning. This enables the project team and the client to understand the risks as a deeper level and to plan mitigation activities and responses accordingly. The higher the risk the greater the associated test and validation is also general required.

Environment

The elements of the project environment include:

- Project management
- Development team
- Client
- Contract
- Process and tools

The environment does not have to "perfect" in order for the Agile mindset in general and specific tools to be useful. However, a less than optimal environment may both slow the adoption of Agile as well as limit its overall effectiveness. Project environmental factors that should be considered assessing for Agile suitability include:

- A large team
- A geographically disperse team
- Waterfall planning methods and processes already in place
- A customer that is either unengaged, unavailable, or both
- Heavy reliance on process and tools that limits willingness to consider alternatives
- Fixed cost and scope

If the majority of project environmental factors are determined to be non-Agile an approach that attempts to leverage Agile specific processes, tools and methods is likely to be ineffective.

Going Agile

Key steps associated with in support of becoming more Agile include:

- Team readiness
  - What is the current state of the team in terms of familiarity and comfort with Agile approaches?
  - Is the team ready to move to Agile practices?
  - What needs to be done to make them ready?
- Customer readiness
  - Who is the customer?

- Is the client prepared to accept and thrive in a project execution and client service delivery environment where they will be an integral part of the design and delivery team?
- Is the client prepared to effectively differentiate between what must be included in order for a release or deliverable to be successful and what is nice to have?
- Are they ready to move to more Agile approaches?
- What needs to be done to make them ready?

- Project Management
  - How ready is the project management team to move to more Agile practices?
  - How ready and able is project management to not accept project plans that specify deliverable dates for first products being many months out?
  - How ready and able is project management to disband approaches that have deliverables being passed from analysts to architects and then architects to developers?
  - How ready and able is project management to integrate testing into the client service delivery process so that it is assured that deliverables provided to client perform as expected and required?
  - How ready and able is project management to emphasize the importance of working code over documentation?
  - How ready and able is project management to create and sustain a project performance and client service delivery environment where

communication and collaboration are essential norms?

- ◦ How able is project management to bring the customer in as an integral part of the project execution and client service delivery process?
- ◦ Is project management able to provide the development team with the clarity, guidance and resources they need to execute against client needs quickly, effectively, and accurately?
- ◦ How able is project management to discontinue a process once it is established it is not providing value to the project execution and client service delivery environment?
- Project performance environment
  - ◦ What are the current risks associated with the project as well as the expectations and needs around its execution?
  - ◦ Which Agile approaches will be used?
  - ◦ How will a move to Agile affect overall risk?
  - ◦ How well is the project environment suited to the potential changes?
  - ◦ How the performance of Agile methods be measured and evaluated?
  - ◦ How will this performance information and data be fed back into the project management approach?
- Organizational management
  - ◦ How ready is organizational management to provide project management with the autonomy, flexibility and support they need to implement Agile practices, methodologies and approaches?

- How will organizational management measure and evaluate the effectiveness of moves to more Agile methods of project execution and client service delivery?

Questions to Consider

1. What methods does your organization currently use to identify and analyze the specific needs of a project and then match them with the project management approach, methods, and tools that best suit them?
2. How is performance in this area measured and evaluated?
3. What are the opportunities for improvement in this regard?
4. What would have to happen in order for these opportunities to become reality?
5. How would improvement in this area affect overall project execution and client service delivery?
6. What role does the size of the project play in selection of the project management approach, methods and tools that will be used?
7. How is performance in this area measured and evaluated?
8. What are the opportunities for improvement in this regard?
9. What would have to happen in order for these opportunities to become reality?
10. How would improvement in this area affect overall project execution and client service delivery?

11. What role does the project type play in the selection of the project management approach, methods and tools that will be used?
12. What role does the project type play in the identification of personnel competencies required to perform and deliver most effectively?
13. How is performance in this area measured and evaluated?
14. What are the opportunities for improvement in this regard?
15. What would have to happen in order for these opportunities to become reality?
16. How would improvement in this area affect overall project execution and client service delivery?
17. What role does project criticality play in the identification and selection of both the project management approach that will be used and the team members who will be involved with it?
18. How is performance in this area measured and evaluated?
19. What are the opportunities for improvement in this regard?
20. What would have to happen in order for these opportunities to become reality?
21. How would improvement in this area affect overall project execution and client service delivery?
22. What role does the environment the project will be performed and delivered in play in both selection of the project management approach and the team members best suited to do it?
23. How is performance in this area measured and evaluated?

24. What are the opportunities for improvement in this regard?
25. What would have to happen in order for these opportunities to become reality?
26. How would improvement in this area affect overall project execution and client service delivery?
27. What role does team readiness play in how your organization leverages existing project management methodologies?
28. How is performance in this area measured and evaluated?
29. What are the opportunities for improvement in this regard?
30. What would have to happen in order for these opportunities to become reality?
31. How would improvement in this area affect overall project execution and client service delivery?
32. What role does team readiness play when the organization is considering or has decided to move to or use a new or different methodology?
33. How is performance in this area measured and evaluated?
34. What are the opportunities for improvement in this regard?
35. What would have to happen in order for these opportunities to become reality?
36. How would improvement in this area affect overall project execution and client service delivery?
37. How does your organization currently communicate its intentions when either

considering or having decided to move to a different project management methodology?

38. How is performance in this area measured and evaluated?
39. What are the opportunities for improvement in this regard?
40. What would have to happen in order for these opportunities to become reality?
41. How would improvement in this area affect overall project execution and client service delivery?
42. How does an organization manage change including resistance when considering or having decided to move to a new project management methodology?
43. How is performance in this area measured and evaluated?
44. What are the opportunities for improvement in this regard?
45. What would have to happen in order for these opportunities to become reality?
46. How would improvement in this area affect overall project execution and client service delivery?
47. Once a project is underway in your organization how do your current project management approaches and methods deal with partially completed work and deliverables?
48. How is performance in this area measured and evaluated?
49. What are the opportunities for improvement in this regard?
50. What would have to happen in order for these opportunities to become reality?

51. How would improvement in this area affect overall project execution and client service delivery?
52. Once a project is underway in your organization how do your current project management approaches and methods deal with extra processes?
53. How is performance in this area measured and evaluated?
54. What are the opportunities for improvement in this regard?
55. What would have to happen in order for these opportunities to become reality?
56. How would improvement in this area affect overall project execution and client service delivery?
57. Once a project is underway in your organization how do your current project management approaches and methods deal with client requests for extra features or functionality?
58. How is performance in this area measured and evaluated?
59. What are the opportunities for improvement in this regard?
60. What would have to happen in order for these opportunities to become reality?
61. How would improvement in this area affect overall project execution and client service delivery?
62. Once a project is underway in your organization how do your current project management approaches and methods deal with task switching?

63. How is performance in this area measured and evaluated?
64. What are the opportunities for improvement in this regard?
65. What would have to happen in order for these opportunities to become reality?
66. How would improvement in this area affect overall project execution and client service delivery?
67. Once a project is underway in your organization how do your current project management approaches and methods deal with situations where project team members are waiting for work?
68. How is performance in this area measured and evaluated?
69. What are the opportunities for improvement in this regard?
70. What would have to happen in order for these opportunities to become reality?
71. How would improvement in this area affect overall project execution and client service delivery?
72. Once a project is underway in your organization how do your current project management approaches and methods address with extra steps (also known as extra motion)?
73. How is performance in this area measured and evaluated?
74. What are the opportunities for improvement in this regard?
75. What would have to happen in order for these opportunities to become reality?

76. How would improvement in this area affect overall project execution and client service delivery?
77. Once a project is underway in your organization how do your current project management approaches and methods address defects in deliverables?
78. How is performance in this area measured and evaluated?
79. What are the opportunities for improvement in this regard?
80. What would have to happen in order for these opportunities to become reality?
81. How would improvement in this area affect overall project execution and client service delivery?
82. Once a project is underway in your organization how do your current project management approaches and methods address the need to stop performing specific project tasks or using project tools or methods that are not working?
83. How is performance in this area measured and evaluated?
84. What are the opportunities for improvement in this regard?
85. What would have to happen in order for these opportunities to become reality?
86. How would improvement in this area affect overall project execution and client service delivery?

The Customer

The Customer

In traditional waterfall or milestone based project management the analysis and requirements definition is completed by or with the help of the users and stakeholders. The development team is then left alone to get the system built on time, on budget and on specification. This is followed by the users and stakeholders reorganizing for testing after the majority of development work have already been completed. Testings' stated purpose is to ensure the system operates to specification. More often than not testing ends up determining if the system operates to specification. When it doesn't it is then sent back to the design and development team for additional work.

Agile development calls for and in fact requires the customer to be available throughout the project lifecycle. Ideally, availability is defined as a collaborative partnership. This includes:

- Representing the interests of the business, users and stakeholders
- Helping drive an iterative planning process
- Assist with requirements refinement issues as they arise

All project management methods make the point that the customer is paramount, their needs being the only reason the project exists in the first place. In reality it can seem the project exists to serve everything but the clients interests. Agile also makes the point the customer is also paramount, number one in that project environment as well. In an Agile project the customer:

- Understands the purpose of the system both as a user and from a more strategic, organizational level
- Is regularly available to the team
- Is willing, able and empowered to make decisions

A highly engaged customer collaborating with a highly engaged development team significantly increases the likelihood of project success. It enables customer requirements to be more clearly defined resulting in more effective design and coding. It also ensures the relevant functionality ends up being designed into the code. In Agile development a team only performs the analysis and requirements definition after the customer has identified the features that are actually required.

Key qualities to look for in a customer include:

- Knowledge and understanding of the business domain
- Understands and appreciates the objectives of the project and what it is intended to achieve
- Has the time and the expertise to work with the project team
- Able to assist the business, users and stakeholders in making decisions
- Is authorized and capable of making timely, informed decisions
- Is not afraid to take responsibility for their decisions
- Is willing to compromise and is not a perfectionist
- Is politically savvy

Customers must also be able to:

- Select the features to be completed before each iteration begins
- Identify individuals within the organization who know the requirements of each feature
- Exercise the authority needed to make the right individuals available to the team
- Quickly and accurately provide answers to urgent questions
- Be prepared and proactive in their communications, knowing what they want to talk about before meeting with the development team
- Realize that direct questions and timely, accurate answers may be needed to compensate for an inability to express or read non-verbal cues.

Questions to Consider

1. What role does the customer play in projects your organization is currently involved in?
2. How is the effectiveness and impact of this aspect on overall project execution and client service delivery measured and evaluated?
3. What are the opportunities for improvement in this regard?
4. What would have to happen in order for these opportunities to become reality?
5. How would improvement in this area enhance overall project execution and client service delivery?
6. How does the client make themselves available during the project lifecycle for projects your organization is currently involved in?

7. How is the effectiveness and impact of this aspect on overall project execution and client service delivery measured and evaluated?
8. What are the opportunities for improvement in this regard?
9. What would have to happen in order for these opportunities to become reality?
10. How would improvement in this area enhance overall project execution and client service delivery?
11. How does your organizations current project management methodologies leverage customer expertise throughout the project lifecycle?
12. How is the effectiveness and impact of this aspect on overall project execution and client service delivery measured and evaluated?
13. What are the opportunities for improvement in this regard?
14. What would have to happen in order for these opportunities to become reality?
15. How would improvement in this area enhance overall project execution and client service delivery?
16. What type of methods, tools and techniques does your organization leverage to maximize collaboration throughout the project lifecycle?
17. How is the effectiveness and impact of this aspect on overall project execution and client service delivery measured and evaluated?
18. What are the opportunities for improvement in this regard?
19. What would have to happen in order for these opportunities to become reality?

20. How would improvement in this area enhance overall project execution and client service delivery?
21. What types of criteria are used to select customers that will enhance project execution on projects your organization is currently involved in?
22. How is the effectiveness and impact of this aspect on overall project execution and client service delivery measured and evaluated?
23. What are the opportunities for improvement in this regard?
24. What would have to happen in order for these opportunities to become reality?
25. How would improvement in this area enhance overall project execution and client service delivery?

People

People

We hear people are the heart, the core of any organization and the foundation of any teams success. This could not be truer for an Agile project. The health of any Agile project is directly tied to the engagement of the members of the project team. As employee engagement goes, so goes the success of the project.

Employee engagement is defined as the willingness of personnel to give more than that what is expected or required of them. Employee engagement is a function of the amount of discretionary effort personnel are willing and able to give. The essentials of creating and sustaining an environment of high employee engagement include:

- Ensuring all members of the team know what is expected of them. This is important because a move to Agile will probably result in changes to work methods for members of the team. It is important team members have a clear understanding of what is expected of them when there is change occurring. In addition, the Agile project performance and client service delivery environment can in and of itself be characterized by change. Changes in the project performance and client service delivery environment will drive changes to team member performance expectations.
- Ensuring all team members have the resources they need to do their jobs. In addition to material resources a key need on Agile team is the need for constant, focused communication and collaboration.

- Ensuring the strengths of all team members are aligned to the maximum extent possible with the work that needs to be done. Strength is defined as the ability to do a specific task to near perfection every single time and to derive personal satisfaction from doing it. This goal is to ensure the willingness and ability of team members to perform is aligned with the specific tasks and activities that need to be accomplished.
- Ensuring all team members are receiving feedback at least on a weekly basis. If you find a team member receiving more negative than positive feedback you need to consider that the person is not aligned with tasks and activities that leverage their strengths.
- Ensuring team members understand how the work they do connects to and supports the larger organization is working to achieve. A person who does not understand how the work they are doing aligns with and supports the greater whole is more likely to see the work they do as just a job.
- Ensuring everyone on the team is committed to quality. A big part of this goes back to setting and sustaining clear expectations.

Highly engaged team members are also much more likely to engage in the behaviors of high functioning teams, including:

- A high level of trust among all team members
- Team members willing to engage in healthy debate, discussion, disagreement, resolution and ultimately focus on results

- A high sustained level of commitment among all members of the team
- A visible level of personnel accountability on the part of every team member to the overall results of the project

Based on this discussion the types of traits, competencies and characteristics effective Agile team members bring to bear include the ability and willingness to:

- Communicate
- Collaborate
- Act with integrity
- Be intellectually honest
- Act with humility
- Demonstrate continuous curiosity

Questions to Consider

1. What is the current level of performance of the members of your team?
2. What are the opportunities for improvement in this regard?
3. What would have to happen in order for these opportunities to become reality?
4. How would improvement in this area enhance overall project execution and client service delivery?
5. What are the key strengths of your organizations project team members as well as the individual members of the project teams?
6. What are the opportunities for improvement in this regard?

7. What would have to happen in order for these opportunities to become reality?
8. How would improvement in this area enhance overall project execution and client service delivery?
9. How are the strengths of project teams and project team members maximized on work your organization is involved in?
10. What are the opportunities for improvement in this regard?
11. What would have to happen in order for these opportunities to become reality?
12. How would improvement in this area enhance overall project execution and client service delivery?
13. How are the weaknesses of the team as well as individual team members minimized in the context of projects your organization is involved in?
14. What are the opportunities for improvement in this regard?
15. What would have to happen in order for these opportunities to become reality?
16. How would improvement in this area enhance overall project execution and client service delivery

Project Initiation

Project Initiation

Traditional project management and applications development processes approach project initiation and planning activities as essential to be performed before a project is given the authority to begin design work. These activities include:

- Creation of a business case
- Missioning and resourcing the project
- Posting a variety of approval gateways and decision points
- Organizing a team, identifying and collecting requirements
- Selecting a technology
- Developing a plan
- Creating a high level architecture

This leads to a number of very important decisions while the project is still in its infancy. This is done to reduce uncertainty, increase efficiency, etc. A key problem is the actual results of all of this effort are often less than stellar when compared with actual project performance.

Agile seeks to strike a balance between the need and desire for certainty and predictability and the need and opportunity for flexibility based on the certainty of change. This goal is Agile is to project enough planning at the beginning of a project to provide the focus and guide the effort of the team on things that matter most to clients. The following actions can be useful in this regard:

- Define the mission of the project

- Gather a list of features
- Develop a plan reflecting the features to be built, estimated build times, and the iteration they will be built in
- Create a baseline architecture as well as models
- Start with the end in mind – asking and answering questions like:
  - What does success look like?
  - What does completion look like?
  - What does being done look like?

Since time and talent are the two most valuable assets on an Agile project the idea of using a single meeting or even a couple of meetings to accomplish multiple upfront planning goals can be invaluable. This type of planning, also known as "Blitz Planning", focuses on:

- Identifying and gathering attendees
- Brainstorming tasks
- Laying out tasks
- Reviewing tasks
- Estimating and tagging tasks
- Sorting tasks
- Developing the working skeleton, identifying the earliest release and revenue points
- Identifying other releases
- Optimizing the project plan to capture other requirements
- Capturing the output

A walking skeleton is the completion of code intended for production that demonstrates a simple function being performed from one end of the system to the other.

Earliest release is the first opportunity users will have to see a working version of the system. Earliest revenue point is the point at which the system will start making or saving the organization money. The sooner the team can get applications to this point the better.

Questions to Consider

1. How are projects in your organization currently initiated?
2. How is the effectiveness and impact of such activity measured and evaluated in your organization?
3. What are the opportunities for improvement?
4. What would have to occur in order for these opportunities to become reality?
5. How would improving in this area affect overall project execution and client service delivery?
6. What are the activities your organization engages in during project initiation?
7. How is the effectiveness and impact of such activity measured and evaluated in your organization?
8. What are the opportunities for improvement?
9. What would have to occur in order for these opportunities to become reality?
10. How would improving in this area affect overall project execution and client service delivery?
11. How is the mission and focus of projects defined for work your organization is involved in?
12. How is the effectiveness and impact of such activity measured and evaluated in your organization?
13. What are the opportunities for improvement?

14. What would have to occur in order for these opportunities to become reality?
15. How would improving in this area affect overall project execution and client service delivery?
16. What purpose does a mission focus serve on projects your organization is involved in?
17. How is the effectiveness and impact of such activity measured and evaluated in your organization?
18. What are the opportunities for improvement?
19. What would have to occur in order for these opportunities to become reality?
20. How would improving in this area affect overall project execution and client service delivery?
21. How is the practice of creating baseline architecture leveraged on projects your organization is involved in?
22. How is the effectiveness and impact of such activity measured and evaluated in your organization?
23. What are the opportunities for improvement?
24. What would have to occur in order for these opportunities to become reality?
25. How would improving in this area affect overall project execution and client service delivery?
26. What are the key outputs of project initiation activity on projects your organization is involved in?
27. How is the effectiveness and impact of such activity measured and evaluated in your organization?
28. What are the opportunities for improvement?
29. What would have to occur in order for these opportunities to become reality?

30. How would improving in this area affect overall project execution and client service delivery

Software Requirements

Software Requirements

The process of researching, identifying, analyzing, documenting and checking required services and constraints is known as requirements engineering. Key elements of requirements engineering include:

- User requirements are statements written and communicated in a natural language. In addition, diagrams are provided to enable understanding of the services the system is required to provide as well as the constraints under which it must function and operate.
- System requirements set out the system services and constraints in detail. The system requirements document, also known as a functional specification, must be precise. The system requirements document may also serve as a contract between a customer and development team. As a minimum it level sets and communicates clear expectations.
- A software design specification is an abstract description of the software design. This is the basis for the more detailed design and implementation'. This specification adds further detail to the system requirements specification.

Software system requirements are often classified as functional or non-functional requirements. The following definitions are useful in this regard:

- Functional requirements are statements of services the system must provide, how the system must react to specific or particular inputs and how the system must behave in specific or particular situations. In some cases the functional requirements may also explicitly state what the system must not do.

- Non-functional requirements are constraints on the services or functions offered by the system. They include the timing constraints, constraints on the development, process standards, etc.
- Domain requirements are those coming from the application domain. They reflect the characteristics of the domain the system will operate in. Domain requirements often include a combination of functional and non-functional requirements.

Methods of identify and determine software requirements include feasibility studies as well as features and user stories and scenarios.

Feasibility Studies

As discussed, requirements engineering involves all activities associated with and in support of creating and maintaining the system requirements document. The four high level requirements engineering process activities are feasibility studies, elicitation and analysis of requirements, specification of requirements, and validation of requirements.

Key questions in the context of feasibility studies are:

1. How would the organization cope if the system weren't implemented?
2. What are the problems with current processes?

3. How would a new system help alleviate these problems?
4. What types of problems could a new system potentially introduced?
5. What direct contribution will the new system make to achieving the business objectives?
6. How will information be transferred to and from other organizational systems?
7. Does the system require technology that has not been previously used in the organization, with this type of problem or opportunity, or both?
8. What must be supported by the system?
9. What doesn't the system need to support?

Features

Agile projects build systems in small blocks of functionality, ultimately providing the customer with value. These blocks or bits of functionality are known as Agile features or user stories.

A feature is a piece of functionality that:

- Represents a customer experience with the system
- Once completed will be accessible to and useable by the customer
- Can be estimated by the project team
- Does not take more than a few weeks to complete

Features help the customer prioritize what they need in the system. This provides the project team with clear direction and expectations on what they need to be working on to continually add value that is important to the customer to the system. Small features and short iterations help ensure

263

the system is regularly being returned to and maintained in a production capable state.

Features and user stories are typically collected and documented on a list. This list based approach is necessary if the customers are going to be allowed and able regularly reprioritize their needs as well as select the functionality they need at the beginning of each iteration.

The value of the ability to reprioritize to the customer cannot be understated. Because each feature represents an individual bit of functionality prioritization can be based on the value of the function, both relative to the business need and relative to the other features on the list. This allows th3e customer as well as the development team to flex to the needs of the business and client service delivery environment. Prioritization can be as simple as assigning the following values to features:

- Must have
- Nice to have
- Add if possible
- Not important

Another approach to feature prioritization is known as MOSCOW which stands for:

- Must have
- Should have
- Could have
- Want to have

Whichever method is prioritization is used, it is vitally important that the entire team, including the customer, developers and project management personnel understand and agree to the meaning's of all terms and methods associated with and in support of prioritization and reprioritization.

Agile also addresses non-functional requirements. The first approach to working with a non-functional requirement is to try to capture it as a separate feature. This allows the non-functional requirement to be subject to the same cost analysis as the rest of the project.

Tasks can be captured as features in an Agile project as well. For example, user input would be considered a task and as such considered as a feature to be captured and documented in an Agile environment. The ability of the system to accept input is another example of a task that would be captured and documented on a features list on an Agile project.

The two examples just discussed also bring another important element of feature analysis to the forefront, that being naming. Naming features focuses on the value and importance of identifying tasks in a manner both meaningful and useful to the customer. This helps to ensure the customer understands the functionality being discussed during planning sessions so they can prioritize work for each iteration and release in a manner that is best aligned with the customer's needs.

User Stories

User stories describe functionality that is considered valuable by the customer, will take no longer that two weeks to develop, and are planned and created by iteration. User stories provide developers with a clear understanding of what the customer is using the software for, how they will be using it, and how it needs to function in order for the customers to be able to use it to best effect.

When it comes to creating and writing user stories, the customer must be on point. First, each story must be written in the language of the business. This enables the customer to recognize and understand the story in terms of how it describes and relates to the work the business does, how it does it, what it uses to do it, what results from doing the work, etc. Because the customer lives in the business environment, they are the ones with the deep knowledge and understanding of these elements. It may be useful to provide some training and coaching to customers on how to write these stories, but ultimately the responsibility needs to be theirs. By writing the stories the customer is going to be positioned to understand them at the level needed to explain them to the development team and ensure what is developed actually meets the business need.

In addition to providing training and coaching to customers on the processes used to develop an their user stories, solution sheets can also be an effective tool in terms of documenting the solutions the developers settle upon to act, create and implement the solutions the stories require.

Solution sheets provide a standardized method to document the proposed or actual solution to a client

266

requirement, be it functional or non-functional. Effective solution sheets provide the following information:

- Summary of proposed or recommend development activity
- Discussion points integral to the functionality. These points cover only the most important and situation specific aspects such as logic flow or an Agile model.
- Statement of unknowns. These are perhaps the most important elements of solutions sheets. The business and development organization needs to be aware of any risks or issues that could impact or impede progress.
- Clarification of boundaries. These enable the team to clarify and specify what it will and will not do.

In order to be of any value selection sheets must be reviewed by their intended audiences. The whole purpose of the solution sheets is to provide a standardized communication tool and vehicle that will enable both understanding on behalf of all parties and ultimately buy in among these same groups.

In addition to being an effective communication tool solution sheets also provide an excellent input into the estimating process. As discussed, Agile is all about understanding what is most important to the customer in terms of functional and non-functional requirements and then aligning the efforts of the developing team against those requirements in such a way that software functionality is added in iterations that enables a production ready version of the application to always be available.

Since planning on Agile projects is typically performed at both the release and iteration levels estimates are typically required for both tasks and features.

The entire team should perform estimates for features. This reduces the potential for bias and skewing that can sometimes occur if a small number of personnel create such estimates.

Estimates for tasks should be created by developers who will actually be creating and writing the code. Other personnel, specifically those who do not have a hand in or contribute to doing the work do not take part in the estimating process. The reason for this is apparent. By actually being accountable for doing the work a person is estimating the time it will take, they are both aware of and more committed to making the deadlines they have set.

The estimates developers come up with reflect several things. First, the estimates reflect the amount of time the developer believes it will take to complete a task. Second, the estimate reflects the level of confidence as well as certainty (or lack thereof) the developer has in the estimate they provide. If uncertainty is high or there is fear that a blown estimate will impose some type of penalty the estimate is likely to be high.

Agile projects often estimate in or are based on a quantity known as ideal time. Ideal time is a measure based on the idea of the developer being able to do their work in an ideal environment free of distraction and interruption. Questions that can provide clarity in this type of situation include:

268

- How long would it take to complete the task if work was performed without interruption?
- How long would it take to complete the task if all required resources were readily available?
- How long would it take to complete the task if the number if nothing out of the ordinary was encountered?

Fear of being wrong, and suffering the consequences of being wrong, can cause bias to creep into estimating activities. Ideal estimates allow developers to give their best estimate without fear of being wrong. The ideal estimate is nothing more than the developer saying "in a perfect world, this is how long it will take to complete this task". This level of clarity enables project management and the team to do everything they can to remove as many obstacles as possible to create as close to a perfect task performance and client service delivery environment as possible.

Scenarios

Scenarios are descriptions of depictions of different types of situations. In the context of software requirements, scenarios are effective in enabling people to relate to and provide real life examples. Compared to abstractions, scenarios allow the user to see how things work and relate to one and other in ways they can readily understand. This enables them to understand what is going on and provide more relevant feedback. Requirements engineers use the information gathered from these discussions to develop actual system requirements.

Scenarios can be particularly useful for adding detail requirements descriptions. They are descriptive examples of how the users interaction with the actual systems, what they need it to do, and what they expect it to provide to them.

Each scenario covers one or at most a small number of related system actions and user interactions. A scenario starts with an outline of the interaction. During elicitation of the scenario details are added to create a complete description of the specific interaction. A scenario can include:

- A system state description at the beginning of the scenario
- A description of the normal flow of events in the scenario
- A description of what can go wrong and how these types of situations are handled
- Information about the other activities which might be going on at the same time
- A description of the state of the system after completion of the scenario

Scenario based elicitation can be carried out informally. In this type of situation the requirement engineer works with stakeholders to identify scenarios as well as capture the details of the scenarios.

Use cases are a specific type of scenario. Gathering use cases is nothing more than a scenario based technique that enables system engineers to work with users to identify and document the specific ways in which they currently use or will need to use a specific system. Like other scenario based requirements gathering work, use cases are completed for the specific tasks and interactions the users have with the system. When modeled in the Uniform Modeling Language these use cases provide the developer with the specific understanding of the system needed to code the functionality in the system.

Questions to Consider

1. What are the current methods your organization uses to identify, collect, analyze and understand customer requirements?
2. How is the impact and effectiveness of these practices measured and evaluated?
3. What are the opportunities for improvement in this regard?
4. What would have to happen in order for these opportunities to become reality?
5. How would improvement in this are affect overall project execution and client service delivery?
6. How are customer requirements reviewed and validated with the customers on projects your organization is currently involved in?
7. How is the impact and effectiveness of these practices measured and evaluated?
8. What are the opportunities for improvement in this regard?
9. What would have to happen in order for these opportunities to become reality?
10. How would improvement in this are affect overall project execution and client service delivery?
11. What role to user stories, features and use cases play in the identification, analysis and validation of customer requirements for projects your organization is currently involved in?

12. How is the impact and effectiveness of these practices measured and evaluated?
13. What are the opportunities for improvement in this regard?
14. What would have to happen in order for these opportunities to become reality?
15. How would improvement in this are affect overall project execution and client service delivery?
16. What is the average amount of time that passes between the identification of requirements and the delivery of functionality to customers that fulfills their needs?
17. How is the impact and effectiveness of these practices measured and evaluated?
18. What are the opportunities for improvement in this regard?
19. What would have to happen in order for these opportunities to become reality?
20. How would improvement in this are affect overall project execution and client service delivery?
21. How are user requirements captured on projects your organization is currently involved in?
22. How is the impact and effectiveness of these practices measured and evaluated?
23. What are the opportunities for improvement in this regard?
24. What would have to happen in order for these opportunities to become reality?
25. How would improvement in this are affect overall project execution and client service delivery?
26. How are user requirements prioritized on projects your organization is involved in?
27. How is the impact and effectiveness of these practices measured and evaluated?

28. What are the opportunities for improvement in this regard?
29. What would have to happen in order for these opportunities to become reality?
30. How would improvement in this are affect overall project execution and client service delivery?
31. How is the customer involved in the prioritization of the needs the project has been chartered to fulfill?
32. How is the impact and effectiveness of these practices measured and evaluated?
33. What are the opportunities for improvement in this regard?
34. What would have to happen in order for these opportunities to become reality?
35. How would improvement in this are affect overall project execution and client service delivery?
36. How does your organizations current project management methodologies address customer functional and non-functional requirements?
37. How is the impact and effectiveness of these practices measured and evaluated?
38. What are the opportunities for improvement in this regard?
39. What would have to happen in order for these opportunities to become reality?
40. How would improvement in this are affect overall project execution and client service delivery?
41. How does your organizations project management methodologies capture task requirements?
42. How is the impact and effectiveness of these practices measured and evaluated?
43. What are the opportunities for improvement in this regard?

44. What would have to happen in order for these opportunities to become reality?
45. How would improvement in this are affect overall project execution and client service delivery?
46. How are user stories and use cases used in the context of your organizations current project management methods to enable and aid in the identification, analysis, and fulfillment of customer requirements?
47. How is the impact and effectiveness of these practices measured and evaluated?
48. What are the opportunities for improvement in this regard?
49. What would have to happen in order for these opportunities to become reality?
50. How would improvement in this are affect overall project execution and client service delivery?
51. What types of tools and methods are used within your current project management methods to bridge between an existing project management approach and those that are believed will be more effective?
52. How is the impact and effectiveness of these practices measured and evaluated?
53. What are the opportunities for improvement in this regard?
54. What would have to happen in order for these opportunities to become reality?
55. How would improvement in this are affect overall project execution and client service delivery?
56. How is the idea and practice of clarification of boundaries leveraged on projects your organization is currently involved in?

57. How is the impact and effectiveness of these practices measured and evaluated?
58. What are the opportunities for improvement in this regard?
59. What would have to happen in order for these opportunities to become reality?
60. How would improvement in this are affect overall project execution and client service delivery?
61. What role does estimating play in projects your organization is currently involved in?
62. How is the impact and effectiveness of these practices measured and evaluated?
63. What are the opportunities for improvement in this regard?
64. What would have to happen in order for these opportunities to become reality?
65. How would improvement in this are affect overall project execution and client service delivery?

The Development Team

The Development Team

Agile development is based on and driven by people who are dedicated to collaboration, communication and continuous learning. When looking for potential members of Agile project teams it is important to search for people who possess these characteristics. Other attributes of high performance Agile team members are:

- Skilled at working with others
- Ability to openly share new ideas, insights and best practices as well as being totally open and responsive to feedback
- A demonstrated openness and receptiveness to change
- The willingness and ability to be totally accountable for ones own performance and results as well as that of the larger team.

Project Management

On traditional projects it can sometimes seem like the project exists to serve the needs of itself first, and the client second. The seemingly endless calls for status updates, updates to project plans, budgets and other documentation, as well as schedules that put the first deliverables several months out from project initiation all contribute to this feeling. Agile approaches the structure and execution of project management a bit differently.

First, management in general focuses on efficiency, reliability, repeatability, predictability and sustainability. Management is considered successful and effective when they are able to deliver the required results when they are needed, at the cost they are budgeted to be delivered at, and to the required level of quality. People who are able to do this consistently are recognized as effective managers. A common thread that runs through effective management is the need for predictability in the performance and client service delivery environment. The problem is that contemporary project execution and client service delivery environments are not nearly as predictable as they once were. Change is constant. Project management methods and tools that were once so effective, like Program Evaluation and Review Technique (PERT), Critical Path Method (CPM) and even the more contemporary Capability Management Model (CMM) are now less so because of their reliance on at least some semblance of predictability in the project execution and client service delivery space.

Agile is client centric. As such, it aligns the mission, method, tools and resources with the client in such a way that it allows the project management method to flex, adjust and adapt to accommodate changes in the clients own performance environment. In this regard the Agile project delivery team can be seen as an extension, or even better, an integral part of the clients overall business performance and service delivery environment. This change in perspective enables Agile project management to shift from the traditional on characterized by monitoring and controlling to one focusing on enablement, facilitation and support.

A key element of success of Agile is project managements receptivity to the needs of the client service delivery team. Instead of traditional project management practices that find the management team acting as an intermediary between the client and developers, Agile exists to ensure the developers are able to get close to the customer and are in fact doing so.

One of the key reasons Agile is successful is that it enables and requires project management to be receptive to the needs of the team. This brings up an important distinction between Agile project execution and that guided by other types of project methodologies. As mentioned, management is all about efficiency, stability, and predictability. Management works well in steady state environments. Today's project execution and client service delivery environments are anything but stable and predictable. Leadership is at its core about change, about the willingness and ability to move forward even though the environment is less than certain. This is what Agile provides.

Agile methodologies vary in terms of how much control a team should have or needs to have over its own activities. However, the one constant across all of the Agile approaches is teams need to have a degree of say and control in the decision making process. Consider the following examples:

- XP calls for teams where each programmer communicates directly with the customer when and where needed. A coach who is also a programmer leads the XP team. Since each team member is empowered and expected to communicate with the customers there may not even be a need for a project manager.
- Crystal allows for teams that vary in structure, ranging from self-managing to process heavy.

These examples bring to mind a couple of additional points. First, consider the competencies team members need to possess in order to operate effectively in this type of environment.

- Waiting for work to be provided by the project manager is replaced by going out, talking with the customer, and figuring out what they need done in terms of what is most important to them
- Back end testing is replaced by testing being conducted as an integral part of each iteration
- Integration moves from being a milestone to an continuous process
- Accountability moves from each individual only being concerned with what they are doing to awareness, concern and involvement with what the entire team is doing
- Information moves from being something that is held onto to something that is shared openly and continuously

Second, consider where the teams involved with projects currently are in their ability and willingness to demonstrate the competencies associated with and in support of Agile delivery. Consider what a change would require for them to be ready to perform effectively in this type of environment. Before you can think about what a move to Agile would mean to the organization you first have to understand what it would require from the people who would be responsible for making it a reality.

The emphasis Agile places on communication means it also requires feedback mechanisms. This enables the team to regularly evaluate itself to determine if its practices are on target, enabling the desired behaviors and performance, and delivering the required results. When soliciting and collecting feedback Agile teams will seek out both qualitative and quantitative information and data. This enables them to assess overall progress, performance and effectiveness of specific practices, identify when things are not working or performing as expected or required and to respond to changes in requirements, the environment, or both.

The short iterations characteristic of Agile are particularly useful in this regard. Timeliness of feedback, be it about people or processes is critical. It allows the person or people receiving the feedback to recall the specific issues being addressed more clearly and makes change more likely. While waterfall or milestone based projects also use reviews and feedback to determine where a project is compared to where it needs to be, the long time lags between issue and feedback can sometime lessen the effectiveness of the feedback. In the context of feedback timeliness enhances relevance and actionability. The iteration based approach of Agile provides more opportunities for feedback, the result being more data points to compare, better understanding of trends, and faster response when change is needed.

The Customer

As discussed, customer engagement and deep involvement with the project is another trademark of Agile based project work and client service delivery. Customer's selected to fulfill this role must be familiar with as well as supportive of the project. They must also be empowered and equipped to make decisions related to software functionality, carry the voice and represent the larger client group being supported, have a vested interest in the successful outcome of the project.

Different Agile methodologies require different levels of customer access and availability. This can range from daily access to an individual who sits with and works right along side with members of the development team. In order to build this type of relationship with the customer the Agile team need to invest in acquainting the client with the Agile methodology and mindset. This upfront effort will help to ensure the customer is comfortable with defining, explaining and planning new element of functionality on a regular basis.

Processes and Tools

The Agile team is responsible for identifying the tools and processes needed based on what will work best for them, their customers, and the outcomes they are working to achieve and deliver. Just as important, these tools and processes should be of the "just enough" variety, just enough being what is needed to provide the structure to achieve the objective and nothing more. Any tool not accepted by the team or goes beyond providing just enough structure is extra baggage. Examples include project plans or other documents having no basis in reality.

However, the Agile team must be sensitive to the fact that while they as a team are working to be processes and documentation light the customer my have difficulty making the transition. The project team and customer must strike a balance that works for everyone. One way to do this is to work to understand why the client wants to continue to use a specific tool, process or set of documentation. They may have valid reasons for doing. Learning how they do business can go a long way to understanding why they do certain things as well as why they do things in a certain way.

The Contract

Another key feature of Agile is its responsiveness to change. However, this flexibility comes at a price. The price can be paid in terms of time and money. Agile projects accept change as a norm in the overall project execution and client service delivery model. Unlike waterfall or milestone based projects, where dates as well as deliverables and their specifications are fixed, Agile projects seek to deliver based on client needs, and the fact is that client needs can change. This flexibility can cost additional time and money in terms of overall project execution. However, these costs are often more than covered by the fact that production ready code is always available.

Rigid contracts can cause both the development team and the client to focus on the wrong things. Specifically, if time to implementation is growing short and there is still a lot of development to be completed the client can sometimes give in and go with what is done and accept they will have to deal with what is missing later. Or the development team can rush through activities at the end of the traditional waterfall or milestone based project plans, like testing, just to get the code out to the client. Either way the originally agreed upon deliverable is missed.

What Agile Is

A development team cannot simply decide on Monday morning that they are now "Agile". Becoming Agile is not about taking on a title a specific set of policies and processes.

Agile starts with the individual. It is a mindset enabled and sustained by a specific set of beliefs and core values. These provide the foundation of the Agile thinking and behavior. When combined with others, this creates an organizational culture that drives the behavior of anyone involved with project execution and project enabled client service delivery. In that regard Agile is characterized by the following elements:

- The willingness and ability to not just "deal" with ambiguity but in many ways to embrace it based on the idea that change provides opportunities to even more effectively align deliverables with what will most benefit the client in the moment
- The ability to engage in continuous self-directed learning on things that matter most to the team member and the organization
- The ability to foster and sustain an organizational culture whose hallmark is trust and continuous communication
- The willingness to view feedback in all its forms as a gift
- Possess a laser like focus on the goal, that being to provide deliverables that are useful to the customer.

When thinking about Agile it is also important to keep in mind that an individual, project team, or organization does not have to become 100% Agile in order to benefit from the values, principles and processes that comprise it. The reality is that not all organizations or teams are suited to be

Agile. The same applies to projects. However, who can argue that any team will not benefit from more effective communication, greater levels of trust, continuous feedback, and on-going learning and development.

With these ideas in mind, consider the following questions in the context of Agile in your organization and among the members of your teams:

Your Development Team

- What is the current level of communication and collaboration on your team?
- Where are members of your team located?
- What is the size of your team?
- How do members of your team feel about continuous learning and development on things that matter to both them and the clients they support?
- How receptive are the members of your team to changing the way they thing about and act towards the work they do and the client they support in response to dynamic and changing conditions?

Your Project Management

- What is the level of communication between those responsible for project management and those responsible for project enabled client service delivery?
- How does project management respond to and support the needs of the project team members?

- What level of say and influence do members of the project team have in terms of the work they do, how they do their work, and how they ultimately serve the clients?
- What types of feedback mechanisms are used to enable members of the project team to both provide and receive feedback?

Your Customer

- Does your customer want to be involved throughout the lifetime of the project?
- Is your customer willing to make themselves available for questions related to requirements and functionality as they arise?

Your Processes and Tools

- How much say does your team have in the selection of processes and tools they use to execute projects in your organization?
- How much say does your team in how they use the processes and tools available to them?

Your Contract

- How much flexibility is there in the dates your project teams work to?
- How much flexibility is there in the budgets assigned to projects your organization is involved in?

Questions to Consider

1. What role does communication and collaboration play in projects your organization is involved in?
2. What methods are used to evaluate the effectiveness and impact of this element on overall project execution and client service delivery?
3. What are the opportunities to improve in this regard?
4. What would have to happen in order for these opportunities to become a reality?
5. How would improvement in this area affect overall project performance and client service delivery?
6. What are the critical enablers of team performance on projects your organization is involved in?
7. What methods are used to evaluate the effectiveness and impact of this element on overall project execution and client service delivery?
8. What are the opportunities to improve in this regard?
9. What would have to happen in order for these opportunities to become a reality?
10. How would improvement in this area affect overall project performance and client service delivery?
11. What is the level of trust among personnel, including customers and stakeholders, on projects your organization is involved with?
12. What methods are used to evaluate the effectiveness and impact of this element on

overall project execution and client service delivery?

13. What are the opportunities to improve in this regard?
14. What would have to happen in order for these opportunities to become a reality?
15. How would improvement in this area affect overall project performance and client service delivery?
16. What is the level of ability and willingness of personnel working on projects in your organization to engage in constructive conflict?
17. What methods are used to evaluate the effectiveness and impact of this element on overall project execution and client service delivery?
18. What are the opportunities to improve in this regard?
19. What would have to happen in order for these opportunities to become a reality?
20. How would improvement in this area affect overall project performance and client service delivery?
21. What is the level of commitment of project team members, stakeholders and customers to the success of their specific areas of responsibility or service delivery?
22. What methods are used to evaluate the effectiveness and impact of this element on overall project execution and client service delivery?
23. What are the opportunities to improve in this regard?

24. What would have to happen in order for these opportunities to become a reality?
25. How would improvement in this area affect overall project performance and client service delivery?
26. What is the level of commitment of project team members, stakeholders and customers to the success of project areas outside of their direct area of responsibility and accountability?
27. What methods are used to evaluate the effectiveness and impact of this element on overall project execution and client service delivery?
28. What are the opportunities to improve in this regard?
29. What would have to happen in order for these opportunities to become a reality?
30. How would improvement in this area affect overall project performance and client service delivery?
31. How well are members of your organization's project teams, including customers and stakeholders equipped to respond to change?
32. What methods are used to evaluate the effectiveness and impact of this element on overall project execution and client service delivery?
33. What are the opportunities to improve in this regard?
34. What would have to happen in order for these opportunities to become a reality?
35. How would improvement in this area affect overall project performance and client service delivery?

36. What is done to personnel working on projects your organization is involved with have clear expectations, resources, development and support they need to be able to do their best work?
37. What methods are used to evaluate the effectiveness and impact of this element on overall project execution and client service delivery?
38. What are the opportunities to improve in this regard?
39. What would have to happen in order for these opportunities to become a reality?
40. How would improvement in this area affect overall project performance and client service delivery?
41. How is the understanding that every increase in team size results in an exponential increase in the number of possible communication links factored into project team and communication planning?
42. What methods are used to evaluate the effectiveness and impact of this element on overall project execution and client service delivery?
43. What are the opportunities to improve in this regard?
44. What would have to happen in order for these opportunities to become a reality?
45. How would improvement in this area affect overall project performance and client service delivery?
46. When faced with the need or opportunity to initiate a project and associated enabling support activities, how is the project management

approach, method and tool kit selected and aligned with the work to be done?

47. What methods are used to evaluate the effectiveness and impact of this element on overall project execution and client service delivery?

48. What are the opportunities to improve in this regard?

49. What would have to happen in order for these opportunities to become a reality?

50. How would improvement in this area affect overall project performance and client service delivery?

51. What role does organizational management play in your organizations overall project management and client service delivery work?

52. What methods are used to evaluate the effectiveness and impact of this element on overall project execution and client service delivery?

53. What are the opportunities to improve in this regard?

54. What would have to happen in order for these opportunities to become a reality?

55. How would improvement in this area affect overall project performance and client service delivery?

56. What is the level of responsiveness of organizational management to the needs of the project delivery team as well as impacted customers and stakeholders?

57. What methods are used to evaluate the effectiveness and impact of this element on

overall project execution and client service delivery?

58. What are the opportunities to improve in this regard?

59. What would have to happen in order for these opportunities to become a reality?

60. How would improvement in this area affect overall project performance and client service delivery?

61. What roles does feedback play in project execution and resulting client service delivery for work your organization is involved in?

62. What methods are used to evaluate the effectiveness and impact of this element on overall project execution and client service delivery?

63. What are the opportunities to improve in this regard?

64. What would have to happen in order for these opportunities to become a reality?

65. How would improvement in this area affect overall project performance and client service delivery?

66. What role do customers play in and on projects your organization is involved in?

67. What methods are used to evaluate the effectiveness and impact of this element on overall project execution and client service delivery?

68. What are the opportunities to improve in this regard?

69. What would have to happen in order for these opportunities to become a reality?

70. How would improvement in this area affect overall project performance and client service delivery?
71. What role does the contract plan, statement of work, project plan or other top level project related documentation play in the planning and execution of projects your organization is involved in?
72. What methods are used to evaluate the effectiveness and impact of this element on overall project execution and client service delivery?
73. What are the opportunities to improve in this regard?
74. What would have to happen in order for these opportunities to become a reality?
75. How would improvement in this area affect overall project performance and client service delivery?

Requirements Validation

Requirements Validation

Requirements validation focuses on ensuring the requirements identified actually define the system the client wants and is expecting. The processes associated with and in support of requirements validation focus on identifying problems with the requirements specification. These are distinct processes since validation is focused on the complete draft of the requirements documents and specification whereas analysis involves working with incomplete requirements.

Requirements validation plays an important role because errors in a requirements document can lead to development errors, which then lead to extensive rework costs. Even if found during testing the costs can be high. If they are not found until the system is placed in service the costs in terms of lost productivity, errors, the need to recode and retest large parts of the system after error correction, etc.

Effective requirements validation focuses on the following areas:

- Validity – a user may believe a system is needed to perform certain functions. Additional thought and analysis may identify new or different functions that are required. Systems often have a diverse set of user groups and client bases. This diversity also extends to the ways similar and different groups use the system. Any list of requirements is ultimately going to represent a compromise among these various groups with their various needs. Checking requirements for validity before coding begins ensures each group is getting the functionality they expect. The core question here is "Will the system do what all of the user groups expect and need it to do, in the manner they expect and need it to do it in?"

- Consistency – documented requirements should not conflict with one and other. Requirements validation in this regard involves checking to ensure that there are not contradictory constraints or that there are different descriptions for the same piece of functionality. The fundamental question here is "Is everyone on the same page in terms of the functionality they expect to see and what they expect and need the functionality to accomplish?"

- Completeness – the requirements document should include documentation that defines all functions and constraints the users of the system intend there to be. The key question here is "Is the system specific complete, accurate and update to date?"

- Realism – using knowledge of existing technology the requirements should be checked to ensure they can actually be implemented. Realism checks should also take the budget and schedule into account for the system under development. The basic question here is "Can we deliver what is being asked for, in the time it is being asked for, at the price the customer is willing to pay for it?"

- Verifiability – writing and documenting system requirements in a consistent manner helps to ensure that everyone involved with the work is operating from the same frame of reference, possesses a shared understanding of what the requirements are saying, and is working from a common understanding of and agreement on what the system needs to do as well as how it needs to perform once implemented. Key considerations in the area of verifiability include:

- ◦ Is the requirement as identified and stated realistically testable?
- ◦ Do the end users of the system understand the requirements?
- ◦ Is the origin of the requirement readily identifiable and clearly stated?
- ◦ Is the requirement adaptable?

Questions to Consider

1. What role does requirements validations play in projects your organization is involved in?
2. What methods are used to measure and evaluate the effectiveness of effort in support of this element?
3. What are the opportunities for improvement?
4. What would have to occur in order for these opportunities to become a reality?
5. How would improvement in this area affect overall project performance and client service delivery?
6. How are customers leveraged in the requirements validation process?
7. What methods are used to measure and evaluate the effectiveness of effort in support of this element?
8. What are the opportunities for improvement?
9. What would have to occur in order for these opportunities to become a reality?

10. How would improvement in this area affect overall project performance and client service delivery?
11. What is necessary for requirements to be considered valid on projects your organization is involved in?
12. What methods are used to measure and evaluate the effectiveness of effort in support of this element?
13. What are the opportunities for improvement?
14. What would have to occur in order for these opportunities to become a reality?
15. How would improvement in this area affect overall project performance and client service delivery?
16. How is consistency enabled on projects that are addressing the needs of multiple client needs?
17. What methods are used to measure and evaluate the effectiveness of effort in support of this element?
18. What are the opportunities for improvement?
19. What would have to occur in order for these opportunities to become a reality?
20. How would improvement in this area affect overall project performance and client service delivery?
21. What is done to ensure completeness of requirements on projects your organization is involved in?
22. What methods are used to measure and evaluate the effectiveness of effort in support of this element?
23. What are the opportunities for improvement?

24. What would have to occur in order for these opportunities to become a reality?
25. How would improvement in this area affect overall project performance and client service delivery?
26. How are realism checks leveraged on projects your organization is involved in?
27. What methods are used to measure and evaluate the effectiveness of effort in support of this element?
28. What are the opportunities for improvement?
29. What would have to occur in order for these opportunities to become a reality?
30. How would improvement in this area affect overall project performance and client service delivery?
31. What is done to ensure verifiability of requirements on projects your organization is involved in?
32. What methods are used to measure and evaluate the effectiveness of effort in support of this element?
33. What are the opportunities for improvement?
34. What would have to occur in order for these opportunities to become a reality?
35. How would improvement in this area affect overall project performance and client service delivery?

System Design

System Design

System design focuses on deciding which capabilities are to be implemented on the software and hardware sides of the architecture. These types of decisions should be left to be made as late as possible in the design process. This allows the design to match the requirements of the performance environment as closely as possible. A good system design process results in a system that can be easily and effectively implemented.

Design patterns are useful vehicles for software design. Design patterns are high level abstractions documenting successful design solutions. They are fundamental to design reuse in object oriented development. A design pattern description should include the name of the patter, a description of the problem as well as the solution, and a statement of the results that can be expected from implementing the solutions as well as the tradeoffs required by using the pattern.

Key design decisions include:

- Partitioning
- Reuse
- User interface
- System interface
- Fault tolerance
- Safety

Even the simplest systems are composed of several hundred lines of code that form objects and modules. These objects and modules interact with the users, one and other,

307

and even other systems and architectures. Because of this complexity systems are always decomposed into subsystems that provide some set of services. The initial design work focuses on identifying and characterizing these subsystems. This allows a framework doe subsystem control and communication to be created. The output of this work is called Architectural Design. Architectural Design is the description of the software architecture.

The architectural design process is focused on establishing a basic structural framework for a system It involves identifying the major components of the system as well as the communication that occurs between the components. Advantages of explicitly designing and documenting software architecture include:

- Stakeholder communication – the architecture is a high level representation of the system. This representation can be used to focus discussion among a wide range of potential stakeholders and users.
- System analysis – making system architecture explicit early in the system development process means that some analysis may be conducted early in the process as well. Architectural design decisions have a profound effect on whether or not the system will be able to meet critical system requirements such as performance, reliability and maintainability.
- Large scale re-use – a systematic architecture is a compact, manageable, understandable description of how a system is organized and how its components interoperate. The architecture can be transferred across systems with similar

308

requirements. This allows it to support system reuse.

The following activities are common to all system architectural design processes:

- System structuring – the system is structured into a number of principle subsystems. A subsystem is an independent software unit. System structuring allows for communication between subsystems to be identified.
- Control modeling – a general model of the control relationships between the parts of the system is established.
- Modular decomposition – each identified subsystem is decomposed into modules. The architect must decide in the types of modules as well as their interconnections.

The system architecture affects the performance, robustness, distributability and maintainability of the system. The particular style and structure chosen for an application can depend on non-functional system requirements such as:

- Performance – if performance is a critical requirement this suggests that the architecture should be designed to localize critical operations within a small number of subsystems with as little communication as possible between these subsystems. This may require the use of relatively "large grain" rather than "finer or smaller grain" components in order to reduce the amount of cross component communication.

- Security – if security is a critical requirement a layered architectural structure should be considered. This will allow the most critical assets to be protected in the innermost layers of the architecture. A high level of security validation for these layers will also add to the security.
- Safety – if safety is a critical requirement the architecture should be designed so that operations related to safety are all located in either a single system or a small number of subsystems. This reduces the costs and problems associated with and in support of safety validation and makes it possible to provide related protection systems.
- Availability – if availability is a critical requirements this suggests the architecture should be designed to include redundant components so it is possible to replace and update components without stopping the system.
- Maintainability – if maintainability is a critical requirement the system architecture should be designed using fine grain, self-contained components that can be readily changed. Producers of data should be separated from consumers of data and shared data structures should be avoided.

Agile Design

With a foundation of system design established, lets turn our attention specifically to Agile design. To start with, let's examine some misperceptions associated with Agile design:

- Less design – a common misconception about Agile is that it is done with less or in some cases without design. Design can be defined as supporting the development of code that meets customer requirements. The reality is that several Agile programming practices are focused on producing better design. These include refactoring, test driven design, and pair programming. In addition, Agile does drive two important features in the design space. First, it greatly reduces the time lapse between design activities and coding. This is achieved through pair programming, better communication and collaboration, clearly defined expectations as well as specifying that whoever does the design also does the coding.
- Less discipline – the reality is that when a person understands and rigorously follows a clear set of expectations and processes they are in fact demonstrating a high level of discipline. This charge could be a result of some not agreeing with the approaches Agile takes. Just because someone does not agree with something does not mean it is undisciplined.

To gain a deeper understanding of Agile design, let's take a deeper look at 8 Agile practices:

- Build automation
- Automated deployment
- Continuous integration
- Simple design
- Collective ownership
- Feature teams

- Refactoring
- Pair programming

Build automation is recognized for its ability to provide the most value per project dollar spent. An automated build reduces the time programmers and developers spend on unnecessary tasks and remove a bottle neck (namely the reliance on one or at best a small number of people to perform a build) from the development process. This enables the development team to respond to changes more efficiently and effectively.

The benefits of an automated build show themselves in a number of ways. First, an automated build frees programmers from performing mundane and repetitive work (the things computers are good at!). This gives them the time to focus on the customer and the code. Second, since any member of the team can perform an automated build the overall response time is reduced. The programmer who makes a change to the code can then make the application ready for redeployment. Third, an automated build that is useable by the entire team reduces the time the team spends chasing down compilation and convergence issues. Within moments of compiling the code the developer knows if it works.

Build automation can be implemented with batch or shell programs or even using a development environment. The advantages gained from a good build tool include the application of an approach that will have already been tested and verified by others, a predefined syntax and structure that helps ensure a set of scripting standards, and the increased potential to reuse proven and validated build frameworks on new projects.

It's important to remember that compile times do matter. Longer compile times (even those as short as 10 minutes) can become a significant impediment to programmers building on a regular basis.

The organizational culture and environment in which the project operates can also put a damper on sharing the build across the entire team. The introduction of an automated build tool can make those who have been responsible for builds up to that point feel threatened. The goal of an automated build tool is not to displace people, it is to enable the team to use their time and skills more effectively. The advantage to an automated build tool is that it is not an "all or nothing" proposition. The team as a whole benefits even if only some of the team members are able to do builds.

Automated deployment is an extension of build automation. The goal of this practice is to streamline and bring predictability to the process of promoting builds from development through testing environments into production.

Automating build deployments provides testers and customers with the latest and best code in less time, minimizes the time the team will spend on this activity, and can also drastically reduce the mix ups that can result from manual build deployment.

User Acceptance Testing (UAT) deployments for teams using a manual build processes are particularly prone to both frustrating errors and hours of lost time. First, there is the possibility no one has done it before. Second, even if the build has been executed previously the coding used for previous builds may be difficult to understand and use for current work. Third, UAT tests can occur at or near the time of delivery when the pressure to deliver is most intense.

It is important to have an agreed upon and documented test process in place that includes both what has to be tested and who will be doing it. In order to achieve maximum effectiveness this work needs to be done early in the development lifecycle. From an Agile development perspective this makes sense. In Agile, the parameters that defined how the code needs to work in production must be defined early. Testing must support what the program needs to do when it is put into production.

Continuous integration focuses on keeping the developers as close as possible to the code, its execution, and ultimately its implementation. It requires developers to focus on if the code works, if the elements integrate properly and if it will ultimately satisfy client needs and expectations.

Continuous integration relies on developers checking their code with the team as they complete small units of functionality. The challenge is that for some developers the benefits of the approach are not readily obvious. This goes back to the idea that a move to Agile is as much a change to organizational culture as it is to specific coding practices. Something that can help individuals with this change is to focus them on the idea that in Agile they are responsible for the entire application, something much broader than specific units, modules, or objects they may have worked on before. Continuous integration helps individual developers understand and appreciate the fact that most important quality measure for any unit of code is how it fits in and works with the broader application the customer has commissioned the team to produce and deliver.

314

Simple design is responsive design. Responsive design is characterized by the ability of the team to make changes quickly, effectively and accurately based on customer needs or changes in the business or performance environment. One approach Agile takes to bring changeability to the process is through the use of short development iterations. In addition to enabling the team to work on only what is known, short iterations also mean that if change does occur, the changes required will impact a smaller set of code than would otherwise be the case if the team used longer build and delivery cycles. Simple design builds onto the idea of speed, quality, and flexibility based on the premise that the simpler something is the easier it is to both maintain and change. Clean, simple code also enables new team members to learn and come up to speed more quickly. It also provides for a more enjoyable work experience in that clean, simple design greatly increases the likelihood the code will work as designed and as needed. Developers like to succeed, and working code is a powerful measure of success. Code should be as complex as it needs to be to accomplish the tasks but no more.

To use simple design the development team should have implemented build automation and automated testing. These practices will allow the developer to write just enough code to complete a new task, compile the code, compile the code, test the code to ensure nothing is broken, and then repeat.

To conclude this discussion on simple design, consider the following:

- Clearly define the problem, opportunity, or objective

- Identify and consider the simplest solution that could possibly work
- If you know you are not going to be using something do not invest anytime working on it
- Do all tasks just once

Collective code ownership addresses the fact that the complete application belongs to and is the responsibility of every member of the development team. This can be a change from other development projects and mindsets the members of the team have been associated with and worked within. On other projects, individual team members may have been responsible for specific elements, modules, or functions. Once they had finished their work on their specific areas of responsibility they handed their work over to an integration team who was responsible for bringing all of the pieces together. Then the work was handed over to the testing team to see if all of the pieces performed as required. If not, the code was sent back to the development team who worked to figure out what went wrong.

Collective code ownership takes a different approach. In this realm, the entire set of code is everyone's responsibility. As such it encourages and enables team members to work in areas they perhaps have not worked in before. Collective ownership fosters more effective development of code as well as faster learning. A primary benefit of collective ownership is a less time wasted and less duplicate code.

Collective ownership means every developer on the team owns every line of code the team produces. There is no "my code" or "your code", only "our code". As such, it can also reduce the inclination or temptation of developers to

316

simply copy and paste the work of one developer to complete a task they are working on. It's fine to copy, but make sure it is the simplest, most effective solution to the problem you are working on.

In order for collective ownership to truly take everyone on the team must be willing to work effectively as a team. This is predicated by trust, the willingness and ability to address conflict and to leverage healthy conflict to enable to the team to higher levels of performance, team accountability and ownership of results. This level of personal accountability to one and other and a genuine focus on results prevents team members from making the mistake of "treading too lightly" on another developers work for fear of creating conflict. Team members operating in the spirit of openness and personal accountability welcome feedback as an opportunity to improve their personal performance and that of the team.

Perhaps the best example of the power of true collective ownership is Wikipedia. Everyone owns the work. The actions of all reflect on each individual, and the work of each individual reflects on the entire team.

Feature teams are characterized by the developers owning and being responsible for the development of specific classes of code and functionality in support of the application. The iterative nature of Agile software development pulls the owners of classes of software related to and in support of a specific feature together. The task of feature teams is to complete specific features in one to two week iterations. Class ownership and feature teams can result in a system that is better designed and easier to maintain than one developed through collective ownership.

317

The proponents of feature teams believe the practice makes the most of class ownership while providing many of the benefits of collective ownership. The following discussion provides some of the key benefits of feature teams in support of Agile development.

- First, when working with feature teams developers typically do not need to wait for other programmers to make changes to code. Under normal circumstances all the programmers with coding responsibilities related to and support of a feature are members of the team assembled to complete the feature.
- Second, feature teams distribute knowledge of the system across the entire project team. Programmers are constantly working within the feature teams alongside other developers who own the classes within the system. Because design sessions and code reviews are performed across everyone of the classes each developer becomes familiar and in many cases very well versed and knowledgeable with many parts of the total system.
- Third, feature teams promote and enable overall better design. Because individual programmers own classes a single programmer is ultimately responsible for keeping the code within the class they are responsible for as clean as possible. There us never a question as to who is responsible for the state of any piece of code within the system.

A project team following features team practices assigns specific roles and responsibilities to different developers on the team. This enables each developer on the team to own one or more classes within the system. This is the enactment of class ownership. Additional features are assigned to owners in a similar manner. Feature owner (also known as Chief Programmers in Feature Driven Development) should be experienced developers. They will be taking on roles and responsibilities similar to those of Chief Programmers. They will typically receive a set of features needing development in support of the larger project. The Chief Programmer is ultimately responsible for the correct design and completion of the features assigned to them.

Feature teams are assembled based on the needs of the development work. The life of a feature team begins with a walk through of the domain and ends with the inclusion of the assigned feature into the larger system build. They are kept together until the work on the features is completed. In order to effectively complete all of the work associated with and in support of the development and delivery of the features assigned to them a features team should never be dependent on the work of others outside of their specific team in order to complete the tasks assigned to them.

Refactoring enables a rigorous application of simple design. It enables developers to implement a sufficient but less than optimal solution today and then consider, develop and implement the tomorrow. It also helps isolate iterations in as little as a week. It also allows the code to be clarified after it has been written.

The three major activities performed when refactoring are:

- Simplifying complex chunks of code
- Replacing similar operations in reusable code
- Removing duplicate code

All of these activities require automated tests in the portion of the code that will be refactored. If there is not sufficient test coverage support refactoring then additional tests should be written before beginning refactoring.

It's important to keep in mind that refactoring is not rework. It is done to improve the functionality and maintainability of code while it is still in design. It is far easier less costly to improve the efficiency and effectiveness of the product before it goes into operation.

Pair programming is based on the fact that developers working in pairs produce better code and fewer errors than developers working individually. While having developers work together can slow down overall development (research shows that paired programming work is approximately 15% slower than individual programming), the time is more than made up for by an equal reduction in errors, additional testing and rework. Pair programming also provides an excellent forum for training new team members as well as mentoring junior team members. It also enables knowledge to spread much faster across the larger development team.

Pair programming begins as soon as two developers partner together to design a piece of code. Each takes the role of either Driver or Partner. The Driver keys while the Partner plays the role of consultant or advisor. The two developers continually switch roles as they move through the work. It can also be effective to pair an analyst or customer with the developer. This partnership enhances the customers understanding of how the application supports their needs as well as enhancing the developers understanding of the specific customer needs.

Questions to Consider

1. What role does design play in projects your organization is currently involved in?
2. How is the impact of this activity measured and evaluated?
3. What are the opportunities for improvement?
4. What would have to occur in order for these opportunities to become reality?
5. How would improvement in this area affect overall project execution and client service delivery in your organization?
6. What is the relationship between design and development (coding) on projects your organization is currently involved in?
7. How is the impact of this activity measured and evaluated?
8. What are the opportunities for improvement?
9. What would have to occur in order for these opportunities to become reality?
10. How would improvement in this area affect overall project execution and client service delivery in your organization?
11. What has to occur in order for a project to move from design to development on projects your organization is currently involved in?
12. How is the impact of this activity measured and evaluated?
13. What are the opportunities for improvement?

14. What would have to occur in order for these opportunities to become reality?
15. How would improvement in this area affect overall project execution and client service delivery in your organization?
16. How is discipline (defined as the willingness and ability of the team to adhere to established guidelines, methods, and processes) applied in the context of projects your organization is currently involved in?
17. How is the impact of this activity measured and evaluated?
18. What are the opportunities for improvement?
19. What would have to occur in order for these opportunities to become reality?
20. How would improvement in this area affect overall project execution and client service delivery in your organization?
21. How is the practice of build automation applied on projects your organization is currently involved in?
22. How is the impact of this activity measured and evaluated?
23. What are the opportunities for improvement?
24. What would have to occur in order for these opportunities to become reality?
25. How would improvement in this area affect overall project execution and client service delivery in your organization?
26. How is the practice of automated testing applied on projects your organization is currently involved in?
27. How is the impact of this activity measured and evaluated?

28. What are the opportunities for improvement?
29. What would have to occur in order for these opportunities to become reality?
30. How would improvement in this area affect overall project execution and client service delivery in your organization?
31. How is the practice of automated deployment applied on projects your organization is currently involved in?
32. How is the impact of this activity measured and evaluated?
33. What are the opportunities for improvement?
34. What would have to occur in order for these opportunities to become reality?
35. How would improvement in this area affect overall project execution and client service delivery in your organization?
36. How is the practice of continuous integration applied on projects your organization is currently involved in?
37. How is the impact of this activity measured and evaluated?
38. What are the opportunities for improvement?
39. What would have to occur in order for these opportunities to become reality?
40. How would improvement in this area affect overall project execution and client service delivery in your organization?
41. How is the practice of simple design applied on projects your organization is currently involved in?
42. How is the impact of this activity measured and evaluated?
43. What are the opportunities for improvement?

44. What would have to occur in order for these opportunities to become reality?
45. How would improvement in this area affect overall project execution and client service delivery in your organization?
46. How is the practice of collective ownership applied on projects your organization is currently involved in?
47. How is the impact of this activity measured and evaluated?
48. What are the opportunities for improvement?
49. What would have to occur in order for these opportunities to become reality?
50. How would improvement in this area affect overall project execution and client service delivery in your organization?
51. How is the practice of feature teams applied on projects your organization is currently involved in?
52. How is the impact of this activity measured and evaluated?
53. What are the opportunities for improvement?
54. What would have to occur in order for these opportunities to become reality?
55. How would improvement in this area affect overall project execution and client service delivery in your organization?
56. How is the practice of refactoring applied to projects your organization is currently involved in?
57. How is the impact of this activity measured and evaluated?
58. What are the opportunities for improvement?

59. What would have to occur in order for these opportunities to become reality?
60. How would improvement in this area affect overall project execution and client service delivery in your organization?
61. How is the practice of paired programming applied to projects your organization is currently involved in?
62. How is the impact of this activity measured and evaluated?
63. What are the opportunities for improvement?
64. What would have to occur in order for these opportunities to become reality?
65. How would improvement in this area affect overall project execution and client service delivery in your organization?

Verification and Validation

Verification and Validation

Verification and validation (V & V) is the name given to the set of activities that ensure software conforms to its specification and meets the needs of the customers it is being created for. V & V starts with requirements reviews and continues through design reviews and code inspections. IV & V concludes with product testing. V & V processes and activities should be integrated throughout the software development cycle. Key elements to attend to include:

- Validation – is the right product being built?
- Verification – is the product being built in the right way?

There are two methods to conduct V&V:

- Software inspections – involves analyzing and checking system representations system representations such as the requirements document, design diagrams, and program source code.
- Software testing – executing on implementation of the system with test data and then examining the outputs of the system and its operational behavior to determine if it performing as required.

The ultimate goal of V&V is to establish confidence the software is fit for use. This does not mean the program must be completely free of defects. It does mean the system must perform correctly for the use it was designed and developed for. The level of confidence depends on the systems purpose, the expectations of the system users and

329

the current marketing environment of the system. Key considerations include:

- Software function – the level of confidence required is dependent on how critical the software is to an organization.
- User expectations – it is becoming ever more rare for customers to be willing to accept "buggy" software or software that does not perform to expressed needs or expectations
- Marketing environment – when software is marketed the sellers of the application must take into account competing packages, prices, features, etc.

Questions to Consider

1. What types of V&V processes, procedures and tools does your organization currently use in support of development projects it is involved in?
2. How is the effectiveness of the methods measured and evaluated?
3. What are the opportunities for improvement?
4. What would have to occur in order for these opportunities to become reality?
5. How would improvement in this area enhance overall project execution and client service delivery?
6. How is software developed by your organization verified?
7. How is the effectiveness of this aspect measured and evaluated?
8. What are the opportunities for improvement?

9. What would have to occur in order for these opportunities to become reality?
10. How would improvement in this area enhance overall project execution and client service delivery?
11. How is software being developed by your organization validated?
12. How is the effectiveness of this aspect measured and evaluated?
13. What are the opportunities for improvement?
14. What would have to occur in order for these opportunities to become reality?
15. How would improvement in this area enhance overall project execution and client service delivery?
16. What role do inspections play in projects your organization is involved in?
17. How is the effectiveness of this aspect measured and evaluated?
18. What are the opportunities for improvement?
19. What would have to occur in order for these opportunities to become reality?
20. How would improvement in this area enhance overall project execution and client service delivery?
21. What role does testing play in projects your organization is involved in?
22. How is the effectiveness of this aspect measured and evaluated?
23. What are the opportunities for improvement?
24. What would have to occur in order for these opportunities to become reality?

25. How would improvement in this area enhance overall project execution and client service delivery?
26. How does your organization determine fitness for delivery and use of product outputs from projects it is currently involved in?
27. How is the effectiveness of this aspect measured and evaluated?
28. What are the opportunities for improvement?
29. What would have to occur in order for these opportunities to become reality?
30. How would improvement in this area enhance overall project execution and client service delivery?

Software Testing

Software Testing

Inconsistent and even poor quality has been the bane of software development for more than 40 years. It was the North Atlantic Treaty Organization (NATO) that realized the strategic implications for national defense that poor software quality brought to bear in 1967. Their response was to begin to professionalize the software development craft. They started by renaming software development to Software Engineering.

The Agile Approach to Testing

The following highlights the differences between Agile approaches to software testing and the more traditional approaches of the Institute of Electric and Electronic Engineers (IEEE).

- IEEE Standard for Software Unit Testing
  - A unit test is a set of one or more computer program modules together with associated control data, usage procedures and operating procedures that satisfy the following conditions:
    - All modules are from a single computer program
    - At least one of the new or changed modules in the set has not completed the unit test
  - The set of modules together with its associated data and procedures are the sole object of the testing process
  - IEEE standards for unit testing
    - Design

- Develop
- Test
  - Plan
  - Determine
  - Refine
  - Design
  - Implement
  - Execute
  - Check
  - Evaluate
  - Deliver
- Agile (Extreme) Standard for Software Unit Testing
  - The developer writes tests method by method, e.g., the tests are written as a precursor to the code being developed
  - A developer writes a test under the following circumstances
    - If the interface for a method is at all unclear you write the test before you write the method
    - If the interface is clear but you can envision the implementation will be the slightest bit complicated you write the test before you write the method
  - Testing in Extreme
    - Select new features
    - Write tests
    - Design and develop code
    - Run tests
    - Deliver

Factors that aid in determining the level of testing required on a project include:

- The criticality of the system
- The desired or required level of system maintainability
- The customers tolerance for error
- The ease or difficulty entailed in redeploying the system

There are several situations that will require a broader perspective when designing and applying tests. They include:

- Sharing a code base with another project team
- Sharing common components with another project team
- Depending on code or components produced by another team

Test Driven Development (TDD)

TDD approaches the task of software development from the perspective that performance criteria will be identified up front, as part of the analysis and design work, before any coding begins. In TDD coding cannot start before the performance criteria are defined because it is the performance criteria that determine at least in part what the design needs to be, what it needs to address, and what it needs to consist of. The very act of writing the tests before the code ensures the code will be testable.

TDD also provides developers with certainty that any updates that are needed and performed can be done so knowing that consideration has been given to the needed updates integrating effectively with existing software. In essence, TDD provides very clear expectations to the developers. They need to develop code that passes the tests that have been written in support of them and that the code will have to pass in order to be considered working code.

Automated Unit Testing

Just as an automated build reduces the amount of time a team spends on compilation and convergence issues, so too will automated testing reduce the amount of time the team spends on identifying and correcting defects.

In Agile, tests are written before coding begins. Tests should be based on all that is known about the environment the application will be running in, the types of inputs it will need to accept as well as the types of outputs it will need to provide, as well as other systems (both hardware and software) it will need to interface with. Sources for this information include user stories and use cases as well as understanding of related software and hardware architectures.

All of this analysis will lead to and support a meaningful understanding of required functionality. The required functionality forms the basis of test development (which then forms the basis of code development in Agile).

Because testing of any kind, but automated testing in particular in Agile, relies on expertise of both the system under development and the other architectures it will interact and interface with, communication, trust and collaboration are essential. Agile relies heavily on the team to accomplish the work that needs to be done to bring the deliverables to the customers. Anything that detracts from that is going to be a potential barrier to meaningful test development and execution.

Acceptance Testing

Acceptance tests are typically used in tandem with features, user stories and use cases. Contrary to common belief about the purpose of testing, the first purpose of acceptance testing is not to identify or snag random defects. Instead, acceptance tests provide a mechanism for the customer to accept a feature by being shown and convinced it works as needed. In this way acceptance tests may also be leveraged to capture and document requirements.

In addition to ensuring the acceptability of features as they are completed, properly implemented acceptance tests carry the following additional benefits:

- With automated acceptance tests the amount of effort spent on testing activities remains steady over time instead of increasing with every new or additional test.
- The number of defects that make it out of development should be reduced significantly.

Acceptance tests provide the greatest benefit when they are specified and written by the customer. The acceptance test for a given user story should test everything a test writer (and ultimately the customer) wants or requires to be verified in order to sign off on the implementation of the code supporting the story. Because tests play such a critical role in development they must be completed early in the overall project, specifically in the analyze and design phases.

While acceptance tests do not have to be written to cover every possible feature or piece of functionality they do need to be written such that when an application passes acceptance testing the customer and development team can be certain of the deliverables readiness and fitness for use.

Questions to Consider

1. What role does testing currently play in your organizations project management and client service delivery environment?
2. How is the effectiveness and impact of this work measured and evaluated?
3. What are the opportunities for improvement?
4. What would have to happen in order for these opportunities to become reality?
5. How would improvement in this area affect overall project execution and client service delivery?
6. Where is testing positioned in your organizations current project management and client service delivery processes?
7. How is the effectiveness and impact of this work measured and evaluated?
8. What are the opportunities for improvement?
9. What would have to happen in order for these opportunities to become reality?
10. How would improvement in this area affect overall project execution and client service delivery?
11. How is the effectiveness and impact of this work measured and evaluated?
12. What are the opportunities for improvement?

13. What would have to happen in order for these opportunities to become reality?
14. How would improvement in this area affect overall project execution and client service delivery?
15. Who in your organization is responsible for testing on projects your organization is currently involved in?
16. How is the effectiveness and impact of this work measured and evaluated?
17. What are the opportunities for improvement?
18. What would have to happen in order for these opportunities to become reality?
19. How would improvement in this area affect overall project execution and client service delivery?
20. What role does the customer play in testing in support of projects your organization is involved in?
21. How is the effectiveness and impact of this work measured and evaluated?
22. What are the opportunities for improvement?
23. What would have to happen in order for these opportunities to become reality?
24. How would improvement in this area affect overall project execution and client service delivery?
25. How are the data and results of testing fed back into the design and development functions of projects your organization is involved in?
26. How is the effectiveness and impact of this work measured and evaluated?
27. What are the opportunities for improvement?

28. What would have to happen in order for these opportunities to become reality?
29. How would improvement in this area affect overall project execution and client service delivery?
30. What methods are currently used to improve the testing processes on projects your organization is involved in?
31. How is the effectiveness and impact of this work measured and evaluated?
32. What are the opportunities for improvement?
33. What would have to happen in order for these opportunities to become reality?
34. How would improvement in this area affect overall project execution and client service delivery?

Small Releases

Small Releases

Releases in an Agile environment begin with the customer identifying a set of factors or user stories for the team to complete and ends with the delivery of that functionality either to the customer for review or into production.

In Agile development the release is generally the largest time box. It is used for planning from a functional scheduling point of view. A key point to keep in mind is that the project itself is not considered a time box in Agile. The project itself is composes of one or more time boxes.

Releases are characterized by the following:

- A group of two or more iterations that share specific start-up or closing activities
- One iteration at the end of a sequence of two or more iterations, the output of which is intended to be production ready even though it may not go into production
- The same as an iteration in which case every completed iteration must be production worthy

Production worthy refers to an ideal state. It is the closest a development team can bring a system to a deployable state at the end of an iteration in support of a release.

Typical release planning activities include:

- Updating the list of work features, users stories or gadgets along with anything that was learned during the previous release as well as any new work.

- Prioritizing the list of work. The customer should complete this step. Developer input should include known risks, dependencies, as well as known unknowns.
- Determine the release data and the amount of work the team can complete.

Sometimes the release date will already be known and fixed while other times the client may have to set it. If known and fixed the focus will be on what features can be completed by the target date and which ones the customer identifies as most important. If the date is set by the client the focus is on what they need. The date is then set based on when the development team can deliver the specified features and functionality.

Projects operating within heavier project management and process environments may find they have engage in requirements tracing. On projects where functionality is based on features or user stories there will be a clear, straight forward relationship and linkage. However, such linkages can be more difficult to find and identify if the requirements are not tied to a specific, well known and well understood requirement. Tracing enables these types of linkages to be visible and understood by all involved with the work. Maintaining a spreadsheet or other similar documentation that shows how features are tied to requirements is a good practice to engage in.

Questions to Consider

1. What types of activities, actions and outcomes characterize releases on projects in your organization?
2. How is the effectiveness of the practice measured and evaluated on in terms of its impact on overall project performance and client service delivery?
3. What are the opportunities for improvement?
4. What would have to occur in order for these opportunities to become reality?
5. How would improvement in this area affect overall project execution and client service delivery?
6. What role do iterations play in projects your organization supports?
7. How is the effectiveness of the practice measured and evaluated on in terms of its impact on overall project performance and client service delivery?
8. What are the opportunities for improvement?
9. What would have to occur in order for these opportunities to become reality?
10. How would improvement in this area affect overall project execution and client service delivery?
11. What role does time boxing play in projects your organization is involved in?
12. How is the effectiveness of the practice measured and evaluated on in terms of its impact on overall project performance and client service delivery?
13. What are the opportunities for improvement?
14. What would have to occur in order for these opportunities to become reality?

15. How would improvement in this area affect overall project execution and client service delivery?
16. How is the term "production worthy" defined and used in the context of projects your organization is involved in?
17. How is the effectiveness of the practice measured and evaluated on in terms of its impact on overall project performance and client service delivery?
18. What are the opportunities for improvement?
19. What would have to occur in order for these opportunities to become reality?
20. How would improvement in this area affect overall project execution and client service delivery?
21. What types of activities characterize release planning on projects your organization is involved in?
22. How is the effectiveness of the practice measured and evaluated on in terms of its impact on overall project performance and client service delivery?
23. What are the opportunities for improvement?
24. What would have to occur in order for these opportunities to become reality?
25. How would improvement in this area affect overall project execution and client service delivery?
26. How do projects your organization is involved in trace and link customer requirements to customer ready deliverables?
27. How is the effectiveness of the practice measured and evaluated on in terms of its impact on overall project performance and client service delivery?
28. What are the opportunities for improvement?

29. What would have to occur in order for these opportunities to become reality?
30. How would improvement in this area affect overall project execution and client service delivery?

350

Executing Iterative Development

Executing Iterative Development

The traditional approach to project execution in support of software development entails an upfront front phased plan broken down into individual task packets which are then rolled up to create a Work Breakdown Structure (WBS) or Gantt Chart. These documents then become the guiding force (aka project plan) that project progress and performance is measured against.

As discussed, Agile advocates a series of short iterations (typically one to eight weeks in length). Each iteration has its own design, build, test and delivery phases built into it. These small iterations lead to regular releases of functionality, enable progress to be tracked at a more reliable level than phased or milestone based approaches, and provide the opportunity for regular feedback from clients to the project team.

Iterations are the time boxes in which Agile projects que up and complete the functionality associated with and in support of entire user stories or sets of features requested by the customer. Scheduling delivery of only complete pieces of functionality is one way Agile enables an iterative process. Other benefits include:

- Allowing a customer to change the direction of a project at the beginning of iteration, queuing up whatever functionality is most relevant and valuable to them at a specific point in time.
- Enabling the prioritization of risk at the beginning of each iteration and based on what the project team has recently learned. This allows the approach and execution to be changed in real time

based on changes that are occurring in the business or client service delivery environment.

- Iterations can ensure a system never strays far from a deployable state since only whole, complete features are planned and delivered within iteration.
- The regular analyze, design, develop, test, and implement cycles that iterations provide for can be used as feedback loops to measure project performance and team productivity and effectiveness.
- Iterations can provide an easy end to a project. This can occur when the customer finds they no longer have a need for any functionality that is currently backlogged awaiting work.

Typical iteration planning activities include:

- Pre-meeting Activities
  o Determine the amount of work the team can complete based on its size, competencies, and resourcing
  o Update the list of work for the release
  o Set a goal for the iteration
  o Select the functionality that will be completed during the iteration and delivered to the client at the completion of it
- Iteration Planning Meeting
  o Present the features the iteration will cover
  o Decompose features into estimated tasks
  o Programmers sign up to complete specific tasks

o   Confirm that commitments are reasonable, both with the individual developers and the entire team

Monitoring Progress Within the Iteration

As mentioned, iterations typically last one to eight weeks. For iterations lasting longer than a week it is useful to monitor progress during the iteration instead of waiting until the iteration is complete to find out what happened.

Project size is a useful guide in determining the level of monitoring that is reasonable or is needed. The larger the iteration in terms of people working or features being worked on the more frequent the meetings should be. When people are very busy a lot can happen in very short periods of time. Agile makes provisions for this type of communication through its use of Scrums and other types of daily "stand ups". These meetings allow everyone on the team to understand the current state of development. This provides leads with the opportunity to reallocate work if needed in order to keep the iteration on schedule. If the team is ahead of schedule it these meetings provide the client with the opportunity to consider adding additional features to the iteration's set of deliverables.

Burn down charts can be useful in providing a visual cue into project status. A **burn down chart** is a graphical representation of work left to do versus time. The outstanding work (or backlog) is often on the vertical axis, with time along the horizontal. That is, it is a run chart of outstanding work. It is useful for predicting when all of the work will be completed. It is often used in agile software development methodologies such as Scrum. However, burn down charts can be applied to any project containing tasks with time estimates.

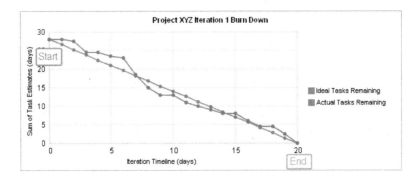

Burn up charts show the amount of work that has actually been delivered.

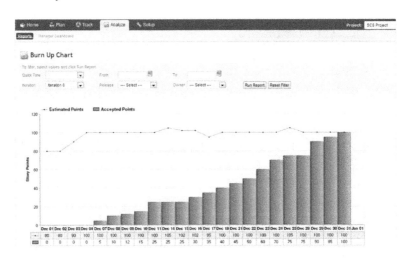

Both are effective in terms of helping the team and the client understand what has been done and what remains to be done on iteration.

Changing the End Date of a Current Iteration

The smaller the iteration the less willing the development team members will be to let the end date slip. This is because moving the end date negates most of the benefit that iteration derives from serving as a time box. However if the end date is allowed to slip a psychological threshold will have been breached. This may cause some members of the team (or the client) to start thinking it is Ok to let other dates slip. This must not be allowed to occur. Firm end dates are in the best interest of the Agile team and the client. They enable and sustain a level of focus and forward movement on the tings that matter most to the customer.

Working Without Iterations

Occasionally a project team may be unable to define a time box suitable to execute an iterative process. This can occur during period of great change or when the technology being used is basically unknown resulting in the feasibility to be in question and the time to complete basically unknowable.

When situations like this arise it is important to still create the best estimates possible based on what is known and the experience of the team members. This enables the team to gain a measure of control over what is going on as well as providing the client with some semblance of an estimate. It is also important to pay close attention to all of the learning the team is going through at this time. This will support closing of the knowledge gap to the point where iteration planning will become viable.

The Task Cycle

The task cycle is a week long iteration like set of activities that enables a more Agile management process to be inserted into a wide variety of project performance and client service delivery environments. Task cycles focus on planning and tracking the work the team has agreed to complete in conjunction with a variety of release level time boxing mechanisms.

Task cycles deliver a lot of the same benefits as well executed one week iterations while at the same time being more versatile. The task cycle is well suited to environments where rapid change is the norm. Many unknowns characterize this type of environment. The introduction of new technologies or heavy use of prototypes can bring this type of uncertainty to the organization. Working in task cycles provides a continuous flow of small but valuable near term goals, frequent assessment of progress, and the opportunity to redirect priorities quickly and effectively.

Key task cycle planning activities include:

- Closing out the tasks in the current task cycle
- Identifying any tasks that were not planned but were completed
- Removing tasks that no longer need to be completed
- Adding new tasks to the list
- Refining estimates
- Determining the amount of time available in the new task cycle
- Selecting the tasks for development
- Determining the owner for each open, active task

Questions to Consider

1. How is project execution carried out on projects your organization is currently involved in?
2. How is the effectiveness of this activity measured and evaluated in the context of overall project execution and client service delivery?
3. What is the current level of performance in this regard?
4. What are the opportunities for improvement?
5. What would have to occur in order for these opportunities to become realities?
6. How would improvement in this area enhance overall project execution and client service delivery?
7. How is project execution aligned with customer needs on projects your organization is involved in?
8. How is the effectiveness of this activity measured and evaluated in the context of overall project execution and client service delivery?
9. What is the current level of performance in this regard?
10. What are the opportunities for improvement?
11. What would have to occur in order for these opportunities to become realities?
12. How would improvement in this area enhance overall project execution and client service delivery?
13. How are customer requests to change direction during project execution handled on projects your organization is involved in?

14. How is the effectiveness of this activity measured and evaluated in the context of overall project execution and client service delivery?
15. What is the current level of performance in this regard?
16. What are the opportunities for improvement?
17. What would have to occur in order for these opportunities to become realities?
18. How would improvement in this area enhance overall project execution and client service delivery?
19. What role does the customer play during iterations and releases?
20. How is the effectiveness of this activity measured and evaluated in the context of overall project execution and client service delivery?
21. What is the current level of performance in this regard?
22. What are the opportunities for improvement?
23. What would have to occur in order for these opportunities to become realities?
24. How would improvement in this area enhance overall project execution and client service delivery?
25. How is project progress assessed in process on projects your organization is involved in?
26. How is the effectiveness of this activity measured and evaluated in the context of overall project execution and client service delivery?
27. What is the current level of performance in this regard?
28. What are the opportunities for improvement?
29. What would have to occur in order for these opportunities to become realities?

30. How would improvement in this area enhance overall project execution and client service delivery?
31. How can the end date be changed on projects your organization is involved in?
32. How is the effectiveness of this activity measured and evaluated in the context of overall project execution and client service delivery?
33. What is the current level of performance in this regard?
34. What are the opportunities for improvement?
35. What would have to occur in order for these opportunities to become realities?
36. How would improvement in this area enhance overall project execution and client service delivery?
37. What is the typical length of iterations or releases on projects your organization is involved in?
38. How is the effectiveness of this activity measured and evaluated in the context of overall project execution and client service delivery?
39. What is the current level of performance in this regard?
40. What are the opportunities for improvement?
41. What would have to occur in order for these opportunities to become realities?
42. How would improvement in this area enhance overall project execution and client service delivery?
43. What role does task cycle planning play in projects your organization is currently involved in?

44. How is the effectiveness of this activity measured and evaluated in the context of overall project execution and client service delivery?
45. What is the current level of performance in this regard?
46. What are the opportunities for improvement?
47. What would have to occur in order for these opportunities to become realities?
48. How would improvement in this area enhance overall project execution and client service delivery?

Reviewing and Tracking Progress

Reviewing and Tracking Progress

What gets measured gets done. Tracking and reviewing progress is all about measurement. Good metrics show both the current stat of the project and provide a means of managing overall performance.

Methods of reporting and tracking progress include:

- Burn down and burn up charts previously discussed
- Performance against target or goal
- Actual performance vs. estimated performance
- Total deliverables passing acceptance tests

Conducting Reviews

Key topics to attend to when conducting reviews include:

- The customer's point of view regarding the current state of development
- The developer's point of view regarding the current state of development
- The overall state of the project team
- The performance of the processes, methods and tools the project team is using in support of their work
- The overall status of the project

As we have discussed frequently throughout is the fact Agile is built on continuous communication and collaboration. Methods of sharing information during reviews include:

- Having every member of the team share what they thought went well on the completed iteration and what could be improved upon in support of the next iteration.
- Having the team prioritize the list of issues coming out of the current iteration and understanding how they might be faced again on the next iteration.
- Developing actionable solutions or ways to address the prioritized issues, working through them until all have been satisfactorily addressed.

Questions to Consider

1. What types of metrics are used to track and report performance of projects your organization is currently involved in?
2. How is the effectiveness and impact of work in this area measured and evaluated?
3. What is the current state of performance in this area?
4. What are the opportunities to improve?
5. What would have to occur in order for these opportunities to become reality?
6. How would improving in this area affect overall project execution and client service delivery?
7. What types of methods, processes and tools are used to report progress and performance of projects your organization is currently involved in?
8. How is the effectiveness and impact of work in this area measured and evaluated?

9. What is the current state of performance in this area?
10. What are the opportunities to improve?
11. What would have to occur in order for these opportunities to become reality?
12. How would improving in this area affect overall project execution and client service delivery?
13. How is project performance data and information used to improve the performance of projects your organization is currently involved in?
14. How is the effectiveness and impact of work in this area measured and evaluated?
15. What is the current state of performance in this area?
16. What are the opportunities to improve?
17. What would have to occur in order for these opportunities to become reality?
18. How would improving in this area affect overall project execution and client service delivery?
19. How are project performance data and metrics used to improve overall performance and client service delivery on projects your organization is currently involved in?
20. How is the effectiveness and impact of work in this area measured and evaluated?
21. What is the current state of performance in this area?
22. What are the opportunities to improve?
23. What would have to occur in order for these opportunities to become reality?
24. How would improving in this area affect overall project execution and client service delivery?
25. What methods, processes and tools are used to conduct project reviews with clients and

stakeholders on projects your organization is currently involved in?

26. How is the effectiveness and impact of work in this area measured and evaluated?
27. What is the current state of performance in this area?
28. What are the opportunities to improve?
29. What would have to occur in order for these opportunities to become reality?
30. How would improving in this area affect overall project execution and client service delivery

Communication and Collaboration

Communication and Collaboration

A hallmark of an Agile performance environment and organizational culture is open, continuous, honest, and straight-forward communication. Agile processes and practices are tuned to work with and compliment the social needs and nature of people as well as the ways effective individuals and teams interact and cooperate with one and other. These processes and practices help programmers develop better habits (such as integrating testing throughout the development process). They also help managers understand and trust the things they hear developers say and see developers do (through the Agile planning, estimation, and execution practices). They enable everyone to focus properly about and on progress (using time boxing to focus on iterations and releases). Finally, Agile is reliant on a health team spirit, one characterized by trust, willingness and ability to engage in healthy conflict, commitment, accountability, and focus on results.

Creating and sustaining such an environment takes work. Methods that can help in this regard include:

- Start by focusing on the needs of the individual team members. High team performance begins with the individual. Key questions include:
  - o Does everyone on the team know what is expected of him or her?
  - o Does everyone on the team have the material, equipment, and resources they need to do their job?
  - o Are the strengths of team members aligned in such a way that provides them

with the opportunity to do what they do best every day?

- o Are team members being recognized for the work they do and the contributions they make on average every seven days?
- o Is the work environment such that all team members believe and feel that someone at work truly cares about them as a person?
- o Are there personnel in the work environment who support the continuous development of team members?
- o Do all members of the team believe there are members of the organization that support and encourage their development?
- o Do all members of the team feel their opinions count?
- o Does the mission and purpose of the organization enable team members to feel and believe their work is important?
- o Do all members of the team understand how the work they do supports the greater objectives the organization is working to achieve?
- o Do all members of the team feel their other team members are committed to doing quality work?
- o Do all team members feel they have a best friend at work?
- o Are team members having meaningful development discussions with their managers at least every six months?
- Strive to make consensus based decisions
- Establish a common area for developers. As discussed, a tenant of Agile is for the

development team to be collocated. When this is possible providing the developers with a common work area greatly increases the opportunity to collaborate. When members of the team can not be positioned in the same physical location, electronic or distance collaboration tools such as Telepresence, Adobe Connect, and Skype can be used to very good effect.

- Ensure important information is available in highly accessible locations in formats usable by all. Given the volume and accessibility needs around information and data today, electronic storage and access is the way to go. Placing such information on shared drives, Wiki's, organizational websites or other areas accessible to everyone on the team are critical. However, it's important to also keep security in mind when creating such locations, providing access, and the information placed and stored there. Examples of information to post include:
    o Work required in support of the current iteration or release
    o Work completed and remaining for the current iteration or release
    o Results of acceptance tests
    o Coding standards
- Institute openness from the top down. A project manager, team lead, or other influential member of the team can have a large impact on the team and how open the members are with one and other. Leaders, both formal and informal, set the tone and culture of communication and collaboration on the team. They do this through their behavior, specifically the manner in which

they engage and respond to individual team members as well as how they encourage team members to respond to each other. In this regard it is important for all team members, including leaders, to understand their own thinking processes, specifically:

- o   What we choose to think about
- o   What we choose not to think about
- o   Why we choose to think about certain things and not others
- o   The manner in which we think about things
- o   The behaviors that our thinking drive
- o   The outcomes resulting from our behaviors
- o   What needs to occur if we find we need to change our thinking in order to achieve something different or achieve in a different way

Agile uses several techniques to keep communication flowing. These include Daily Stand-up meetings and Daily Scrums.

Daily Stand-up meetings bear this name because the attendees stand during the entire meeting. The result is the meetings are kept short, focused, and to the point. Good stand-ups have a rhythm about them, where one person at a time speaks, a few questions are exchanged, issues may be documented for follow-up, then the next person speaks. Stand-ups are all about connecting people with each other. Questions asked and answered during a stand-up include:

- •   What did you complete yesterday?

- What will you be working on today?
- What roadblocks are you facing?
- What do you need to do the work you need to do?

While stand-ups are a good place to identify problems they are not the place to solve them. Solutions should be addressed outside of the stand-up. The reason is that a stand-up will rarely surface an issue that affects the entire team. Why take the time of the entire team to talk about things that do not affect them?

Much like the daily stand-up the Scrum focuses on a quick daily discussion of progress, works to surface issues and obstacles, and moves non-essential discussions (those that do not affect the entire team) to other forums. In addition, the Scrum is a bit more structured than the stand-up. Participants are also able to sit during it.

The Scrum allows the team to continually refine us alignment with the client and overall delivery process. It also helps keep everyone informed on tracking progress and completion of work. The Scrum is also an excellent venue to discuss obstacles that are preventing or blocking the team in terms of achieving its goals.

Questions to Consider

1. What is the current state of communication and collaboration on projects your team is involved in?
2. What methods are used to measure and evaluate the performance and effectiveness of this element?

3. What is the current state of performance in this area?
4. What are the opportunities for improvement?
5. What would have to occur in order for these opportunities to become a reality?
6. How would improving in this area affect over project execution and client service delivery?
7. What methods are used to enable and sustain project related communications on projects your organization is involved in?
8. What methods are used to measure and evaluate the performance and effectiveness of this element?
9. What is the current state of performance in this area?
10. What are the opportunities for improvement?
11. What would have to occur in order for these opportunities to become a reality?
12. How would improving in this area affect over project execution and client service delivery?

Documentation

Documentation

During my career with the United States Air Force I had the opportunity to be involved with system acquisition. My tour with acquisition command took place during the 1980's. Waterfall project management, based on specific project performance milestones and supporting decisions, was the norm. There was a running joke that said a weapon system could not go operational until the weight of the paperwork at least equaled the gross weight of the operational system. In my case the system was the C-17 aircraft. With a maximum takeoff weight of 585,000 pounds we were going to have to generate a lot of paperwork to meet that threshold. I am here to say I believe we did!

Traditional waterfall and milestone-based projects are often "documentation heavy". Although both Agile and waterfall project approaches share similar steps the differences in how those steps are implemented results in different documentation requirements. Let's start by looking at how documentation flows on a typical waterfall or milestone based project.

The process begins with the business case. This is supported with documentation that profiles the rationale for the project as well as high level objectives, schedule, resource and budget requirements, and expected benefits. Identification and analysis of system requirements follows, with its associated documentation. This is followed by the development of system architecture. In addition to the specific system requirements, change documentation also comes into play. System architecture flows into system design, which is followed by development, testing, etc. As mentioned, change documentation flows along with other supporting process documentation.

Project documentation is designed to achieve several objectives (and hence the reason for such large amounts of it). Those objectives include:

- Providing a means of communication among all personnel involved with the project (management, stakeholders, customers, development team members, etc.)
- Providing management and other affected personnel with a record of decisions
- Provide an audit trail to enable personnel to determine if the project results were worth the effort and resources expended to achieve them
- Provide a means of providing control over project activities

A key reason traditional projects carry so much documentation with them is because the documentation must serve a variety of needs for a variety of individuals and groups.

Agile approaches documentation a bit differently. A guiding principle for Agile projects is to have just enough documentation to provide what is needed, no more, no less. This approach is in sync with the overarching Agile philosophy of developing deliverables that just meet the needs of the customer, no more, no less. If you don't know how much this is there are a couple of ways to approach it. First, you can start from scratch and enable the team to identify and specify what is needed. Second, if documentation is already in place, go through it with the team (including customers, stakeholders, and all other affected and interested personnel). Get everyone's perspective on:

- What the documentation is
- If it is used
- What is used for
- How it is used
- When it is used
- What would cause people to stop using it
- What would happen if it was not used

Answers to these questions will quickly help identify which documentation is needed and which can be dropped.

Some basic guiding principles regarding documentation (and Agile development in general) are:

- What is the simplest thing that will work, e.g., simple in terms of use, maintainability, etc.?
- Do you need it?
- What will happen if it is gone?
- Keep information in only one document and in one place
- Ensure one person owns and is responsible for each document. Many people may have input into the document, only one should be responsible for ensuring the document is accurate and complete

Methods of Managing Documentation

1. Seek an alternative solution to the documentation. Is there some other, more effective and efficient way to capture the data and information? Is there

some other more effective and efficient way to make the data and information accessible to everyone who needs it?

2. Who uses it and what do they use it for? Would it be more effective and efficient to require the user of the data and information to be responsible for it?

3. Break out documentation as separate work. If the customer requires heavy documentation it can be effective to break it out and align it with the work it is related to and include the time required to do it in the time estimate. The more time spent on documenting the less time will be spent on coding. As mentioned, the client expectation at the end of an iteration is production quality code that does what they need and expect it to do.

4. Incorporate documentation into tools the team is already using.

5. Use a Wiki.

6. Get the customer to take responsibility for it. Agile is all about delivering production ready code. If something isn't helping achieve this then it is hurting it. Sometimes the customer is in the best position to perform non-development tasks.

Documentation at the Start of the Project

Start-up documentation has its merits. The process can help the team define where it is going and how generally it plans on getting there. Useful techniques include:

- Defining a mission or metaphor for the team. Specifically, why does the team exist, what is it seeking to achieve, how will it know it has achieved success. The mission or metaphor can provide a filter through which all the decisions the team makes must pass. If the idea or task under consideration does support the mission it does not get done.

- A simple but rigorous set of mission artifacts.
    - o Project charter including vision
    - o Project data sheet
    - o Product specification outline.
- Model everything at a high level.
- Complete set of solutions sheets.

Design Documentation

Different styles of Agile leverage different types of design documentation. For example, XP uses a bare minimum of design documentation while FDD requires a sequence of diagrams that supplement the overall model. The difference between the two approaches can be characterized this way. XP provides the development team with an overall focus on what the system needs to do. The team is then left to figure out the best and most effective way to code it to enable it to perform the functions required by the customer. FDD specifies the features the system must contain. The aggregation of the features into the larger system will provide the customer with the required functionality. Once features are defined the development team is then charged to determine the best way to code it. Here are two methods of creating design documentation supporting Agile:

- Executable documentation – many Agile developers share the opinion that executable documentation (consisting of code and tests) is the best method for documenting the system.

Executable documentation entails code written in a simple, easy to understand fashion. It uses self-describing variable and method names. This method assumes the team that writes the tests writes them well and thoroughly covers the system. This can work well if the developers writes the test first, then the code it supports (also known as test driven development).

- In-code commenting – in-code commenting involves place comments (e.g., explanation, descriptions, definition, rationale, etc.) in with the code while it is being developed. A challenge with this method is that as code is updated the comments may be ignored.

Rationale and Structure Document

Many Agile teams will try to maintain a single document that provides an overview of and insight into the entire system. This provides a single comprehensive source of system information, provided it is kept current and up to date.

Project Plan

Traditional waterfall and milestone based project management methods make heavy use of a work breakdown structure (WBS). The challenge is that by design an Agile program can move so fast (with its one to eight week iterations) that maintaining a WBS can become very difficult and non-value adding.

A List of Work to be Done (LWD) is a method that enables understanding the work to be done in association with the overall client service delivery schedule.

To create an effective LWD:

- Begin with a complete list of the tasks and activities associated with and in support of the work that needs to be done.
- Draft the overall project schedule using a calendar based scheduling method.
- Map the tasks and activities to the calendar-based schedule.
- Add more detail as needed.

Document Handoffs

Document handoffs are the process of passing documents from one group to another. This is done to allow them to review, proof, approve or sign-off on them, among other things. The presence of document sign-off processes can be a sign of less than Agile processes at work.

Documentation can all too often replace the conversations people would be having otherwise. Given the amount of data and information flowing around people are far less likely to attend to a document and review it to the level needed than they are to pay attention to a conversation. Documentation that summarizes the outcomes of a conversation is fine, but using documents to take the place of conversations will slow the overall execution down.

Adding Documents

Before creating or adding a new document consider the following:

- What will be in it?
- Who will use it?
- When will it be used?
- How often will it be used?
- When will it require updating?
- Who will be responsible for updating?
- How will it be updated?
- Is there enough time in the schedule to handle these requirements?
- Is there another way to satisfy the need for information that does not include documentation?

Questions to Consider

1. What role does documentation play on projects your organization is involved in?
2. How is the effectiveness of this activity measured and evaluated?
3. What is the current level of performance in this area?
4. What are the opportunities for improvement?
5. What would have to occur in order for these opportunities to become a reality?
6. How would improving in this area affect overall project performance and client service delivery?
7. What methods are used to manage documentation for projects your organization is involved in?
8. How is the effectiveness of this activity measured and evaluated?

9. What is the current level of performance in this area?
10. What are the opportunities for improvement?
11. What would have to occur in order for these opportunities to become a reality?
12. How would improving in this area affect overall project performance and client service delivery?
13. What triggers the creation of documentation on projects your organization is involved in?
14. How is the effectiveness of this activity measured and evaluated?
15. What is the current level of performance in this area?
16. What are the opportunities for improvement?
17. What would have to occur in order for these opportunities to become a reality?
18. How would improving in this area affect overall project performance and client service delivery?
19. What triggers updates to documentation on projects your organization is involved in?
20. How is the effectiveness of this activity measured and evaluated?
21. What is the current level of performance in this area?
22. What are the opportunities for improvement?
23. What would have to occur in order for these opportunities to become a reality?
24. How would improving in this area affect overall project performance and client service delivery?
25. What triggers decisions to discontinue using specific documentation on projects your organization is involved in?
26. How is the effectiveness of this activity measured and evaluated?

27. What is the current level of performance in this area?
28. What are the opportunities for improvement?
29. What would have to occur in order for these opportunities to become a reality?
30. How would improving in this area affect overall project performance and client service delivery?
31. Who controls the decisions on stopping the use of specific project documentation on projects your organization is involved in?
32. How is the effectiveness of this activity measured and evaluated?
33. What is the current level of performance in this area?
34. What are the opportunities for improvement?
35. What would have to occur in order for these opportunities to become a reality?
36. How would improving in this area affect overall project performance and client service delivery?
37. How is the importance of specific categories and types of documentation determined for projects your organization is involved in?
38. How is the effectiveness of this activity measured and evaluated?
39. What is the current level of performance in this area?
40. What are the opportunities for improvement?
41. What would have to occur in order for these opportunities to become a reality?
42. How would improving in this area affect overall project performance and client service delivery?

Quality Management

Quality Management

Software quality is seen by some as a complex topic that defies easy definition. I disagree with this. I define software quality as conformation to specification, or does the software do what it needs to do, in the manner in which it needs to do it, when it needs to do it, with what it needs to do it with. The better the software conforms to the specifications the higher the quality. However, there are a few challenges associated with this definition when applied to software development:

- The software specification should be oriented towards the characteristics of the product the customer wants. However, the development organization may also have requirements (such as maintainability) that are not included in the specification.
- We do not know how to specify certain quality characteristics (such as maintainability) in an unambiguous way.
- It is very difficult to write complete software specifications. Although a software product may conform to its specification its users may not consider it to be a quality product

Quality managers are responsible for ensuring required levels of quality are achieved. In principle quality management simply involves defining standards and procedures that should then be used during software development by all involved in the work.

Good quality managers also work to institute and sustain a "quality culture". They encourage and support their teams in taking responsibility for the quality of their work and ensuring that what is delivered to the customer meets their expectations and specifications.

Software quality management is structured into 3 principal activities:

- Quality assurance – the establishment of a framework of organizational procedures and standards that lead to and sustain higher levels of quality.
- Quality planning – the identification and selection of appropriate procedures and standards form the framework and the adoption of these for a specific software project.
- Quality control – the definition and enactment of processes that ensure project quality procedures and standards are followed by the software development team.

Quality management should be separated from project management so that quality is not compromised by management responsibilities for project budget and schedule. An independent individual or team should be responsible for quality management. The reporting line should be to a level above the project management team.

Software quality attributes include:

- Safety
- Security
- Reliability
- Resiliency
- Understandability

- Testability
- Adaptability
- Modularity
- Complexity
- Portability
- Usability
- Reusability
- Efficiency
- Learnability

Reviews play an important role in software quality management. Reviews of software process deliverables are the most widely used technique for assessing software quality. It is also important to know there are no standardized of universally applicable software quality metrics. Organizations must identify and select those metrics they believe will best suit the needs of requirements of the deliverables they are working to provide to their clients.

Questions to Consider

1. What is your organizations attitude towards quality management in the context of projects it is currently involved in?
2. What methods are currently used to measure and evaluate the effectiveness and impact of this practice in your organization?
3. What is the current level of performance?
4. What are the opportunities for improvement?
5. What would have to occur in order for these opportunities to become reality?
6. How would improvement in this area affect overall project execution and client service delivery?

7. How does your organization implement quality management practice on projects it is currently involved in?
8. What methods are currently used to measure and evaluate the effectiveness and impact of this practice in your organization?
9. What is the current level of performance?
10. What are the opportunities for improvement?
11. What would have to occur in order for these opportunities to become reality?
12. How would improvement in this area affect overall project execution and client service delivery?
13. How does your organization approach the need to embed a quality culture in support of projects it is involved in?
14. What methods are currently used to measure and evaluate the effectiveness and impact of this practice in your organization?
15. What is the current level of performance?
16. What are the opportunities for improvement?
17. What would have to occur in order for these opportunities to become reality?
18. How would improvement in this area affect overall project execution and client service delivery?
19. How does your organization approach quality assurance in support of projects it is involved in?
20. What methods are currently used to measure and evaluate the effectiveness and impact of this practice in your organization?
21. What is the current level of performance?
22. What are the opportunities for improvement?

23. What would have to occur in order for these opportunities to become reality?
24. How would improvement in this area affect overall project execution and client service delivery?
25. How does your organization approach quality planning in support of projects it is currently involved in?
26. What methods are currently used to measure and evaluate the effectiveness and impact of this practice in your organization?
27. What is the current level of performance?
28. What are the opportunities for improvement?
29. What would have to occur in order for these opportunities to become reality?
30. How would improvement in this area affect overall project execution and client service delivery?
31. How does your organization approach quality control in support of projects it is current involved in?
32. What methods are currently used to measure and evaluate the effectiveness and impact of this practice in your organization?
33. What is the current level of performance?
34. What are the opportunities for improvement?
35. What would have to occur in order for these opportunities to become reality?
36. How would improvement in this area affect overall project execution and client service delivery?
37. How does your organization select the quality attributes it will attend to in the context of projects it is involved in?

38. What methods are currently used to measure and evaluate the effectiveness and impact of this practice in your organization?
39. What is the current level of performance?
40. What are the opportunities for improvement?
41. What would have to occur in order for these opportunities to become reality?
42. How would improvement in this area affect overall project execution and client service delivery?
43. Which quality attributes does your organization consider most important in the context of projects it is involved in?
44. What methods are currently used to measure and evaluate the effectiveness and impact of this practice in your organization?
45. What is the current level of performance?
46. What are the opportunities for improvement?
47. What would have to occur in order for these opportunities to become reality?
48. How would improvement in this area affect overall project execution and client service delivery?
49. Which quality attributes does your organization feel are least important in the context of projects it is involved in?
50. What methods are currently used to measure and evaluate the effectiveness and impact of this practice in your organization?
51. What is the current level of performance?
52. What are the opportunities for improvement?
53. What would have to occur in order for these opportunities to become reality?

54. How would improvement in this area affect overall project execution and client service delivery?

Conclusion

Conclusion

Agile is about building and delivering software that is "just good enough". While this may sound trite, think about it this way. How much of the software that is delivered today is "just good enough". By "just good enough" we mean software that matches our expectations and needs and is fit for use. In that regard you can think of Agile as being an approach that enables the team to deliver quality software.

Agile does this by first enabling the team to get as close as possible to the customer. In Agile customer needs and expectations are the cornerstone of enabling the team to design, develop and delivery production ready software. Second, Agile focuses the team attention on what is known. Based on developing an understanding of customer needs through use cases and user stories, features are identified. The development focuses on designing, developing and delivering the code that supports the required features. Third, by breaking the development work down into short iterations, the level of intensity is maintained at a manageable pace while at the same time enabling changing requirements to be integrated into future development.

Moving to Agile is not an "all or none" proposition. In fact, introducing elements of Agile into existing project management and client service delivery models and methods should be managed as any organizational change or change to processes, methods, and tools would be. With that in mind, who can deny that enabling the client to be a more active member of the project delivery team could provide substantial benefit. The same is true of working off crystal clear expectations as well as actively working to reduce unnecessary documentation.

When it comes right down to it Agile is a set of tools. Like any set of tools it is only as effective as its suitability to the task and the skill of the people using it.

Glossary

Acceptance Testing. Formal testing conducted to determine whether or not a system satisfies its acceptance criteria and to enable the customer to determine whether or not to accept the system.

Adaptability. The ability and willingness of personnel to recognize the need and / or opportunity to adjust to changing circumstances and then taking the necessary steps to do it.

Agile. An approach to project management design to provide the user, client or customer with just enough functionality to meet their needs and expectations, noting more, nothing less.

Agile Development Practices. Procedures and techniques used to conduct Agile software development. Although there is no canonical set of Agile practices, most Agile practitioners adopt some subset of SCRUM and XP.

Agile Manifesto. A philosophical foundation for effective software development, the Agile Manifesto was created by representatives Extreme (XP), SCRUM, DSDM, Adaptive Software Development, Crystal, Feature-Driven Development, Pragmatic Programming, and others sympathetic to the need for an alternative to documentation-driven, heavyweight software development processes.

Agile Model. A model that is just good enough. This means that it fulfills its purpose and no more; is understandable to its intended audience; is simple; sufficiently accurate, consistent, and detailed; and investment in its creation and maintenance provides positive value to your project.

Agile Modeling (AM). A practice-based methodology for effective modeling of software-based systems.

Agile Modeling Session. A modeling session where you follow the principles, and apply the practices, of AM.

Agile Project Management. The style of project management used to support Agile software development. SCRUM is the most widely used Agile project management practice. XP practices also include practices that support Agile project management. Essential feature of Agile project management include Iterative development cycles, Self-organizing teams, Multi-level planning, Dynamic scope, Frequent collaboration with customer and/or business sponsors

Agile Software Development. Features of Agile software development include a heavy emphasis on collaboration, responsiveness to change, and the reduction of waste throughout the development cycle. Agile software development (ASD) focuses on keeping code simple, testing often, and delivering functional bits of the application as soon as they're ready

Alignment. Organizations with production dependencies across department boundaries run the risk of falling out of phase (or alignment). Alignment includes any actions or policies that exist so that a process or activity in one section of the organization is congruent with the organization's or business unit's governing mission. The lack of business/IT alignment

for many organizations and frequently the root cause of systemic software delivery failure.

Analysis Modeling Session. A modeling session where your focus is on fleshing out the requirements for your system.

Analysis Paralysis. The fear of moving forward until your models are perfect.

Analyst. A developer responsible for working directly with project stakeholders to potentially gather/elicit information from them, documents that information, and/or validates that information.

API. Application programming interface.

Application Lifecycle Management. A continuous process of managing the life of an application through governance, development and maintenance.

Architecture Modeling Session. A modeling session where your focus is on identifying a high-level strategy for how your system will be built.

Artifact. A deliverable or work product.

Backlog. A list of user features and stories that needs to be completed.

Baseline. A tested and certified version of a deliverable representing a conceptual milestone which thereafter serves as the basis for further development and that can be modified only through formal change control procedures. A particular version becomes a baseline when a responsible group decides to designate it as such.

BDUF. Big Design Up Front.

Behavioral Requirement. A category of requirements that describe how a user will interact with a system, how someone will use a system, or how a system fulfills a business function.

Bottleneck. Any resource or process whose capacity is less than or equal to the demand placed on it, thus constraining the flow of work or information through the process.

Boundary Object. An object that represents user interface elements such as screens, reports, HTML pages, or emails

Branching. The duplication of objects under revision control (such as a source code file, or a directory tree) in such a way that the newly created objects initially have the same content as the original, but can evolve independently of the original.

Breaking the Build. When a developer adds changes to the source code repository that result in the failure of a subsequent build process, the developer has "broken the build." Avoiding breaking the build is a commitment generally required by agile software developers and integral to the XP practice continuous integration . The build is broken if the build process cannot successfully completed for any number of reasons including (but not limited to) failure to compile, compiling with unacceptable warnings, or the failure of any number of (usually) automated software tests. The more comprehensive the build process, the higher the threshold for breaking the build. If a code submission does result in breaking the build, the developer should immediately remove the cause. If the build breaks but the immediate cause is not self-evident, a frequent practice of established agile development teams is to take immediate action to fix the build.

BUFD. Big Up-front Development

Build Process. The amount of variability in implementation makes it difficult to come up with a tight definition of a Build Process, but we would say that a Build Process takes source code and other configuration data as input and produces artifacts (sometimes called derived objects) as output. The exact number and definition of steps depends greatly on the types of inputs (Java versus C/C++ versus Perl/Python/Ruby source code) and the type of desire output (CD image, downloadable zip file or self-extracting binary, etc.). When the source code includes a compiled language then the Build Process would certainly include a compilation and perhaps a linking step.

Business Rule. An operating principle or policy that your software must satisfy.

Cardinality. Represents the concept "how many?" in associations.

CASE. Computer-aided system engineering.

409

CASE tool. Software that supports the creation and manipulation of models of software-oriented systems.

Catalysis. A next generation software process for the systematic business-driven development of component-based systems.

Change Agent. A person, group, or team who not only believes in the changes being brought forth but also are also actively involved in work focused on making them a reality.

Change Case. An artifact used to describe a potential requirement for a system or a potential modification to existing requirements.

Change Management. Change is a process that involves stopping or dropping the way in-which things are currently being done, accepting and learning the new approach, and then putting the new learning and associated thinking and behavior into action. Understanding change is a process allows the emotional and intellectual barriers and enablers that can affect willingness and ability to change to be addressed in a way that makes the change occur faster and more effectively.

Change Readiness. The willingness and ability of an individual or group to accept change and begin thinking and acting in the new manner. Because change creates uncertainty and resistance it is important for change initiatives to address the emotional and intellectual needs of those being impacted by the change.

410

Class diagram. A UML diagram that depicts classes, their static inter-relationships (including inheritance, aggregation, and association), and the operations and attributes of those classes.

Class Responsibility Collaborator (CRC) card. A standard index card that has been divided into three sections, one indicating the name of the class that the card represents, one listing the responsibilities of the class, and the third listing the names of the other classes that this one collaborates with to fulfill its responsibilities.

Class Responsibility Collaborator (CRC) model. A collection of CRC cards.

Client. The person, people, or organization for which the deliverables are being created.

Cohesion. The degree of relatedness within an encapsulated unit (such as a component or a class).

Collaboration Diagram. A UML diagram that show instances of classes, their interrelationships, and the message flow between them. Collaboration diagrams provide a birds-eye view of a collection of collaborating objects working together to fulfill a common purpose.

Collaborative Modeling Tool. A CASE tool that enables several developers to simultaneously work on one or models with real-time updates of those models.

Collaborative writing tool. A word processing tool that enables several people to simultaneously write a

411

document with real-time updates of that document.

Communication. The act of transmitting information between individuals.

Complexity. A situation characterized by having many parts combined in a series of intricate relationships.

Component Diagram. A UML diagram that depicts the software components of a system, their interfaces, and the relationships between the components.

Connascence. Between two software elements, A and B, the property by which a change in A would require a change to B to preserve overall correctness within your system.

Context Model. A diagram showing how your system fits into its overall environment. It is common to develop high-level data flow diagrams or deployment diagrams for this.

Continuous Integration. Aims to improve software quality and to reduce the time taken to deliver it, by replacing the traditional practice of applying quality control after completing all development.

Contract Model. A model that defines an agreement between two or more parties. A contract model is something that the parties should mutually agree to and mutually change over time if required. Contract models are often required when an external group controls an information resource that your system requires, such as a database, legacy application or information service.

412

Control object. An object that serves as the glue between boundary/interface objects and entity objects, implementing the logic required managing the various objects and their interactions.

Constraint. A restriction on the degree of freedom you have in providing a solution.

Cohesion. The degree of relatedness within an encapsulated unit (such as a component or a class).

Customer. The individual or group for whom the deliverables are being created.

Daily Meeting / SCRUM. A status check where the team meets and share progress, impediments and short term assignments. Usually three questions asked: "What did you do yesterday?", "What will you do today?" and "What is blocking progress?".

Data Domain. A collection of related data entities and the relationships between those entities. Most data domains are based on a common theme or concept within your business domain, such as customer, account, brokerage, and insurance within a financial institution.

Data Model. A diagram that depicts data entities and their inter-relationships.

Data-Flow Diagram (DFD). A diagram that shows the movement of data between processes, entities, and data stores within a system.

Death March. A doomed software project, without any

413

apparent hope of success, where the developers carry on anyway.

Definition of Done. The criteria for accepting work as completed. Specifying these criteria is the responsibility of the entire team, including the business. Generally, there are three levels of "Done" (also known as Done-Done-Done): Done: Developed, runs on developer's box, Done: Verified by running unit tests, code review, etc., Done: Validated as being of deliverable quality with functional tests, reviews, etc.

Deliverable. An artifact that is delivered as part of your overall system. Examples include source code, user documentation, and technical system documentation for operations and maintenance personnel.

Deployment diagram. A diagram that depicts a static view of the run-time configuration of processing nodes and the components that runs on those nodes.

Design modeling session. A modeling session where your focus is on identifying a detailed strategy for building a portion of your system.

Design Pattern. A design pattern is a general reusable solution to a commonly occurring problem in software design

Developer. Anyone directly involved in the creation of a software development artifact. People in the roles of programmer, modeler, and tester are examples of developers.

Development Team. Developers + active project stakeholders.

Document. Any artifact external to source code whose purpose is to convey information in a persistent manner.

Documentation. Persistent information written for people that describe a system, including both documents and comments in source code.

Documentation Handoff. This occurs when one group or person provides documentation to another group or person.

Domain Model. A model depicting major business classes or entities and the relationships between them. It is common to use a class diagram or data diagram for this purpose.

Drawing Tool. A software tool that supports the ability to draw diagrams. Drawing tools are effectively low-end CASE tools.

DSDM. Dynamic Systems Development Method.

Efficiency. The extent to which time and resources are used for an intended purpose and the extent to which the application of the resources allows attainment of a specific objective.

Employee Engagement. The amount of discretionary effort team members are willing to give and put into the work that needs to get done. The higher the level of engagement the greater the performance of the team.

Enterprise Architectural Modeling. The act of creating and evolving models that depict the business and technical infrastructure of your organization.

Enterprise requirements modeling. The act of creating and evolving models that reflect the high-level requirement of the organization.

Entity Object. An object that is typically found in your domain model, for example Order and Item in an inventory control system.

Essential Use-Case. A simplified, abstract, generalized use case that captures the intentions of a user in a technology and implementation independent manner.

Essential user interface prototype. A low-fidelity model of a portion of the user interface for a system in a technology independent manner.

EUP. Enterprise Unified Process

Executable Documentation. The combination of executable code and its supporting tests.

Executable UML (xUML). Strategies in which systems are modeled using the artifacts of the UML and a formal language such as the OCL from which working software is generated.

Executive Overview. A definition of the vision for the system and a summary of the current cost estimates, predicted benefits, risks, staffing estimates, and scheduled milestones.

416

Facilitator. Someone responsible for planning, running, and managing modeling sessions.

Fail Fast. A property of a system or module with respect to its response to failures. A fail-fast system is designed to immediately report at its interface any failure or condition that is likely to lead to failure.

Feature Driven Development (FDD). The act of designing and developing architecture and associated elements, modules, components, etc. that enables the system to perform in specific ways, at specific times, etc.

Feedback. The act of providing activity specific information to an individual or team.

Fibonacci Sequence. A sequence of numbers in which the next number is derived by adding together the previous two (e.g. 1, 2, 3, 5, 8, 13, 21, 34...). The sequence is used to size stories in Agile estimation techniques such as Planning Poker.

Flow Chart. A diagram depicting the logic flow of a business process or software operation. Flow charts are a primary artifact of structured/procedural modeling.

Glossary. A collection of definitions of terms that are relevant to your project.

Graphical User Interface (GUI). A style of user interface composed of graphical components such as windows and buttons.

Hardware Node. A computer, switch, printer, or other

417

hardware device.

In-Code Commenting. The act of integrating code documentation (comments, rationale, logic, etc.) in with the code itself.

Increment. The difference between two releases of a system.

Information Radiator. A display of information posted on the wall where passersby can see it.

Interface. In Java, a collection of zero or more operation signatures that a class implements in whole.

Interface Object. See boundary object.

IT. Information Technology.

Iterate. To move on to the next step/task, often in a repetitious manner taking small steps each time.

Iteration. A term referring to a distinct sequence of activities with a baselined plan and valuation criteria resulting in a release (either internal or external).

Iteration Backlog. A list of user stories and bugs that should be implemented in defined iteration.

Iteration Burndown. Chart showing daily progress during the iteration. It may forecast real iteration end date and display scope creep (added user stories during the iteration).

Ivory Tower Architecture. Architecture developed in

418

isolation from the developers, or teams of developers, responsible for following it.

Joint Application Development (JAD). A structured, facilitated meeting in which modeling is performed by a group of people. JADs are often held for gathering requirements or for modeling candidate architecture(s).

KISS. Keep it simple stupid.

Landscape model. See overview model.

Layering. The organization of software collections (layers) of classes or components that fulfill a common purpose.

Lean / Kanban. Kanban promotes flow and reduces cycle-time by limiting WIP and pulling value through in a visible manner: There are no iterations: only now. Work at the pace you can truly sustain. "Done" means it is in the user's hands. Nothing less. Limit the Work in Progress (WIP). This forces you to get things done, or you'll have nothing else to do. Pull value through (with WIP limit), Make it visible (Visual Control), Increase throughput, Fixed Kanban Backlog, Quality is embedded in (not inspected in)

Learnability. The capability of the software to enable the user to learn how to use it.

List of Work to be Done (LWD). Document that shows the work to be done mapped to a schedule.

Major User Interface Element. A large-grained item such as a screen, HTML page, or report.

Measurement. The act of gauging the performance of a specific attribute against a specific standard.

Message-Invocation Box. The long, thin, vertical boxes that appear on sequence diagrams which represent invocation of an operation on an object or class.

Metric. A quantitative element of measurement.

Minimum Marketable Feature. The smallest set of functionality that must be realized in order for the customer to perceive value. A "MMF" is characterized by the three attributes: minimum, marketable, and feature. A feature is something that is perceived, of itself, as value by the user. "Marketable" means that it provides significant value to the customer; value may include revenue generation, cost savings, competitive differentiation, brand-name projection, or enhanced customer loyalty. A release is a collection of MMFs that can be delivered together within the time frame.

Minor User Interface Element. A small-grained item such as a user input field, menu item, list, or static text field.

Mission. The reason the team exists, focusing on what the team is expected to achieve and how it will know when it is successful.

Model. An abstraction that describes one or more aspects of a problem or a potential solution addressing a

420

problem. Traditionally, models are thought of as zero or more diagrams plus any corresponding documentation. However non-visual artifacts such collections of CRC cards, a textual description of one or more business rules, or the structured English description of a business process are also considered to be models.

Modeling Session. An activity where one or more people focus on the development of one or more models.

Modularity. A continuum describing how elements of components of a system can be separated and recombined.

Multiplicity. The UML combines the concepts of cardinality and optionality into the single concept of multiplicity.

Network Diagram. A model that depicts the various types of hardware nodes and the interconnections between them.

Non-Behavioral Requirement. A category of requirements that describe technical features of a system, features typically pertaining to availability, security, performance, interoperability, dependability, and reliability.

Normalization Data. A data modeling technique, the goal of which is to organize data elements in such a way that they are stored in one place and one place only.

Normalization Object. An object modeling technique, the goal of which is to organize behavior in such a way that it is implemented in one place and one place only.

Note. A modeling construct for adding free-form text to UML diagrams.

Object Constraint Language (OCL). The industry standard specification language defined by the Object Management Group (**www.omg.org**).

Object lifeline. Represents, in a sequence diagram, the life span of an object during an interaction.

OOA&D. Object-oriented analysis and design. OOA&D should be considered activities, not phases.

Optionality. Represents the concept "do you need to have it?" in associations.

Operations Documentation. This documentation typically includes an indication of the dependencies that your system is involved with; the nature of its interaction with other systems, databases, and files; references to backup procedures; a list of contact points for your system and how to reach them; a summary of the availability/reliability requirements for your system; an indication of the expected load profile of your system; and troubleshooting guidelines.

Organization Chart. A model that depicts the reporting structure between the people, positions, and/or teams within an organization.

Osmotic Communication. Indirect information transfer through overhearing conversations or simply noticing things happening around you.

Overview Diagram. A high-level depiction of one aspect of your system's architecture. Any type of diagram, such as a UML class diagram or a data model, may be used as an overview diagram when appropriate for the given view.

Phase Modeling sessions. A modeling session where your focus is on creating models pertinent to the major phases of traditional development. This includes but is not limited to requirements, analysis, architecture, and design modeling sessions.

Physical Prototype. A physical model of the actual environment in which a system is to be deployed.

PIG. Process improvement group (the pun is intended).

Planning Poker. Planning Poker is a consensus-based technique for estimating, mostly used to estimate effort or relative size of tasks in software development

Portability. The characteristics that enable a piece of software to be moved from one system to another.

Process. A series of two or more tasks or activities that when performed accurately and in the proper sequence lead to a specific outcome.

Product Backlog. A list of customer requirements for the entire product.

Process Object. See control object.

Product Vision. A product vision is a brief statement of the desired future state that would be achieved through the project initiative. The product vision may be expressed in any number of ways including financial performance, customer satisfaction, market share, functional capability, etc. The product vision is typically the responsibility of executive sponsorship and is articulated to the Agile development team by the business and by the product owner, if the team is using SCRUM.

Production Ready. Deliverables ready to be put to work in actual production. The client does not have to put them into production in order for them to be considered production ready, they just have to be able to if they chose to.

Project Overview. A document that summarizes critical information such as the vision for the system, primary user contacts, technologies and tools used to build the system, the critical operating processes (some applicable to development, such as how to build the system and some applicable to production, such as how to back up data storage), and references to critical project artifacts such as the source code, the permanent models, and other documents. This document serves as a starting point for anyone new to the team.

Project Plan. Document profiling the specific tasks and activities associated with and in support of project execution, including dates, resource requirements, and overall schedule.

Project Stakeholder. A direct user, indirect user, manager, senior manager, operations staff member, support (help desk) staff member, testers, developers working on other systems that integrate or interact with this one, or maintenance professionals potentially affected by the development and/or deployment of a software project. For the sake of Agile Modeling developers working on the project shall be excluded whenever the term "project stakeholder" is used, even though they clearly have an important stake in the projects that they work on.

Quality. Conformance to specification. The tighter the conformance the higher the quality.

Quality Assurance. The establishment of a framework of organizational procedures and standards, which lead to and sustain higher levels of quality.

Quality Control. The definition and enactment of processes, which ensure project quality procedures and standards, are followed by the software development team.

Quality Culture. An organization characterized by a continual focus on designing and delivering programs, products and service that possess the conformance to specification the customer seeks.

Quality Planning. The identification and selection of appropriate procedures and standards form the framework and the adoption of these for a specific software project.

Rationale and Structure Document. A single

comprehensive source of information covering the entire system.

Refactoring. disciplined technique for restructuring an existing body of code, altering its internal structure without changing its external behavior undertaken in order to improve some of the non-functional attributes of the software. Typically, this is done by applying series of "refactoring's", each of which is a (usually) tiny change in the code that does not affect its functionality. Advantages include improved code readability and reduced complexity to improve the maintainability of the source code, as well as a more expressive internal architecture or object model to improve extensibility.

Release. The deployment of a working version of a system. Releases may be internal, available only to the development team, or external, available to some or all of the users for the system.

Release Backlog. A list of user stories, features and bugs that should be implemented in defined release.

Release Burndown. Chart showing implementation progress during a release. It provides answers on the following questions: When release could be completed based on previous progress? What progress has been made in previous iterations? Is our velocity good enough to complete the release on time?

Release Planning. The goal of a release planning meeting is to create release plan. During release planning all user stories estimated, prioritized and likely assigned to specific release. In many cases just few releases

426

planned ahead and other user stories put into backlog.

Reliability. The ability of a person or system to perform and maintain its functions in routine circumstances, as well as hostile or unexpected circumstances

Resilience. The ability of a system to absorb an external shock and still continue to perform as needed and as designed.

Requirements Document. This document defines what the system will do, summarizing or composed of requirements artifacts such as business rule definitions, use cases, user stories, or essential user interface prototypes (to name a few).

Requirements Modeling Session. A modeling session where your focus is on defining what your project stakeholders want your system to do.

Requirements traceability matrix. The artifact used to record traceability relations between artifacts.

Retrospective. A time boxed meeting held at the end of an iteration, or at the end of a release, in which the team examines its processes to determine what succeeded and what could be improved. The retrospective is key to an Agile team's ability to "inspect and adapt" in the pursuit of "continuous improvement." The Agile retrospective differs from other methodologies' "Lessons Learned" exercises, in that the goal is not to generate a comprehensive list of what went wrong. A positive outcome for a retrospective is to identify one or two high-priority action items the team wants to work on in the next iteration or release. The emphasis is on actionable items, not comprehensive analysis. Retrospectives may take many forms, but there is usually a facilitator, who may or may not be a member of the team, and the process is typically broken down into three phases: data gathering, data analysis, and action items.

Reusability. The likelihood a segment of source code that can be used again to add new functionalities with slight or no modification. Reusable modules and classes reduce implementation time, increase the likelihood that prior testing and use has eliminated bugs and localizes code modifications when a change in implementation is required.

Robustness. The persistence of a system's characteristic behavior under perturbations or conditions of uncertainty.

Robustness Diagram. A model that depicts the major objects – classified into boundary/interface objects, entity objects, or control/process objects – that participate in fulfilling an actor's interaction with a system as defined by a usage scenario.

RUP. Rational Unified Process

Safety. The state of being free from threats.

Scribe. A person responsible for recording information during a modeling session.

Scrum. An Agile meeting method enabling team members to share task and function specific activity updates with the team.

Security. Degree of protection from danger.

SEPG. Software engineering process group.

Sequence Diagram. A UML diagram used to explore the logic of usage scenarios.

Software Development Artifact. See artifact.

Software Reviews. A process or meeting during which a software product is [examined by] project personnel, managers, users, customers, user representatives, or other interested parties for comment or approval

Source Code. A sequence of instructions, including comments describing those instructions, for a computer system. Also known as program code, program source code, or simply as code.

Specification Language. A style of writing, such as Object Constraint Language (OCL) and Structured English, used to describe logic in a structured/formal manner.

Sponsor. The individual, group, or organization that approves the project and provides the resources required for its successful execution.

SPI. Software process improvement.

Spike. A story or task aimed at answering a question or gathering information, rather than implementing product features, user stories, or requirements. Sometimes a user story is generated that cannot be estimated until the development team does some actual work to resolve a technical question or a design problem. The solution is to create a "spike," which is a story whose purpose is to provide the answer or solution. Like any other story or task, the spike is then given an estimate and included in the sprint backlog.

Sprint. The SCRUM term for an iteration. The sprint starts with a sprint planning meeting At the end of the sprint there is a sprint review meeting, followed by a sprint retrospective meeting.

Sprint Planning Meeting. Each sprint begins with a two-part sprint planning meeting, the activity that prioritizes and identifies stories and concrete tasks for the next sprint. For a one-month or four-week sprint, this two-part meeting should last eight hours; for a two-week sprint, it lasts about four hours. As a general rule of thumb, the number of weeks in a sprint multiplied by two hours equals the total length of the spring planning meeting. Part one of the sprint planning meeting is a review of the product backlog. This is when the product owner describes what needs to be built for the next sprint. During this part of the meeting, it is not uncommon for the team to discuss the sprint objectives with the product owner, and ask clarifying questions and remove ambiguity. During part two of the sprint planning meeting, the team decides how the work will be built. The team will begin decomposing the product backlog items into work tasks and estimating these in hours. The product owner must be available during this meeting but does not have to be in the room. The output of the second planning meeting is the Sprint Backlog.

Sprint Review. A meeting held at the end of each sprint in which the SCRUM team shows what they accomplished during the sprint; typically this takes the form of a demo of the new features. The sprint review meeting is intentionally kept very informal. With limited time allocated for Sprint review prep. A sprint review meeting should not become a distraction or significant detour for the team; rather, it should be a natural result of the sprint.

SRS. Software Requirements Specification.

Stakeholder. An individual or group with an interest in the project and its outcomes. Stakeholders can be categorized as 1) those whose support is needed and who will be positively impacted by the project outcomes, 2) those who support is needed and who will be negatively impacted by the project, 3) those whose support is not needed but will be positively impacted by the project and 4) those whose support is not needed and who will be negatively impacted by the project.

Stand-up Meeting. An Agile meeting method enabling team members to share task and function specific activity updates with the team.

State chart diagram. A UML diagram used to depict the various states that an object may be in and the transitions between those states.

Stereotype. A UML stereotype denotes a common usage of a modeling element. Stereotypes are used to extend

431

the UML in a consistent manner.

Structure Diagram. A diagram that depicts the modules of procedure-based code and the invocation relationships between those modules.

Structured English. A traditional, easy to read, style of specification language.

Support Documentation. This documentation includes training materials specific to support staff; all user documentation to use as reference when solving problems; a trouble-shooting guide; escalation procedures for handling difficult problems; and a list of contact points within the maintenance team.

System. The software, documentation, hardware, middleware, installation procedures, and operational procedures.

System documentation. The purpose of this document is to provide an overview of the system and to help people understand the system. Common information in this document includes an overview of the technical architecture, the business architecture, and the high-level requirements for the system.

System Requirements. Clear definition of what the system must do in order to successfully meet client needs and requirements.

System Use Case. A use case in which high-level implementation decisions are reflected, such as the specific type of user interface and your physical environment.

432

Technical Debt. Describes the obligation that a software organization incurs when it chooses a design or construction approach that's expedient in the short term but that increases complexity and is more costly in the long term. Whether or not to incur technical debt is a tradeoff decision that ideally is made in a deliberate manner at the point that work occurs.

Technical Requirement. A requirement pertaining to a non-business-related aspect of your system, such as a performance-related issue, a reliability issue, or technical environments issue.

Testability. The capability of a system to be tested.

Test Case. Set of criteria that define what the deliverable must do, how it must do it, when it must do it, what it must do it with, and what is expected based on what it does.

Test Driven Development (TDD). The act of writing the test the code will have to pass in order to ensure it meets client needs and then writing the code. The thinking is that if the code passes the test (which is based on customer requirements) it will perform, as the client needs it to once it is in production.

Testing. Activity associated with and in support of determining if what has been designed performs in the expected and / or required manner.

Time-boxing. The act of identifying specific blocks or "boxes" of time, normally one to eight weeks, and then specifying the work that will be completed during them.

Traceability. The ease of which the features of one artifact – perhaps a document, model, or source code – are related/traced to the features of another.

Truck Insurance. The assurance that if the development team leaves, or gets hit by a truck, that critical information about the project is left behind in the form of documentation.

Truck Number. An estimate of minimum number of people you would need to lose from your team before you find yourself in trouble (e.g. the number of people that would need to be hit by a truck).

UML. Unified Modeling Language.

Understandability.

UP. Unified Process.

Usability. The extent to which something can be learned and used for the purpose for which it was designed.

Usage Scenario. A description of a single path of logic through one or more use cases or user stories.

Use Case. A sequence of actions that provide a measurable value to an actor.

Use Case Diagram. A UML diagram used to depict a

collection of use cases, actors, their associations, and optionally a system boundary box.

Use Case model. The combination of one or more use case diagrams and the supporting use cases and actor definitions.

User Documentation. Documents describing how to work with your system, including reference manuals, usage guides, support guides, and training materials.

User Interface (UI). The portion of software that a user directly interacts with.

User Interface Element. See major user interface element and minor user interface element.

User Interface Flow Diagram. A diagram that enables you to model the high-level relationships between major user interface elements, depicting a birds-eye view of the user interface of your system.

User Story. A reminder to have a conversation with your project stakeholders that captures a behavioral requirement, a business rule, a constraint, or a technical requirement.

Version Control Tool. A software tool used to check in/out, define, and manage versions of project artifacts.

Virtual Meeting Tool. A tool that enables communication between several people in different physical locations.

Vision. The ideal state, what absolute success looks like.

Voice of the Customer. Voice of the Customer (VOC) is a term used in business and Information Technology (through ITIL) to describe the in-depth process of capturing a customer's expectations, preferences, and aversions. Specifically, the Voice of the Customer is a market research technique that produces a detailed set of customer wants and needs, organized into a hierarchical structure, and then prioritized in terms of relative importance and satisfaction with current alternatives.

WIP. Work In Progress

Work Product. A type of artifact, such as a model or project schedule, that you create during development that you may discard or evolve into an actual deliverable.

Work Breakdown Structure (WBS). Tool used in waterfall and milestone based approaches to project management that shows the specific tasks and activities that need to be accomplished, the sequence they need to be accomplished in, the amount of time required for them, all integrated into an overall calendar based schedule.

Working Software. Software that has been tested, accepted by its users, and then released.

XP. eXtreme Programming

xUML. See Executable UML.

YAGNI. You Ain't Gonna Need It Anyway

436

The Back Story

My professional career began in August of 1980 when I enlisted in the United States Air Force. While in the military, I had the opportunity to serve in a variety of operational and support positions including aircraft maintenance, logistics, systems acquisition, troop readiness and professional military education. I retired from the Air Force in November of 2000 at the rank of Chief Master Sergeant.

I transitioned to the private sector that same year. My first position after retiring from the service involved supporting technical and operations training in the financial services industry. From there I have had the opportunity to work in a variety of project management, consulting, engineering, training development, and human performance enablement roles. I currently serve as a corporate VP supporting leadership development for technology professionals.

My interest in leadership and performance development and improvement began with my Air Force enlistment. The service provided me with the opportunity to work for and learn from some of the best of the best in these areas. Writing professionally represents the next step in my personal development in this area as well. I have long been a believer that if you want to really learn how to do something well teach someone else how to do it. By extension, I have found that you can deepen your understanding and ability through writing.

I am a true believer in the value and importance of continuous development. Towards that end, I carry a variety of degrees, including a Master's in Aerospace Science (MAS) from Embry Riddle Aeronautical University as well as a Master of Arts (MA) in Organizational Leadership and a Master's in Business Administration (MBA) from Northcentral University. My professional certifications include Professional in Human Resources (PHR) from the Society for Human Resource Management (SHRM) and Project Management Professional (PMP) from the Project Management Institute (PMI) as well as Six Sigma Black Belt.

Perhaps most important, I view every day as a development opportunity, full of those unavoidable opportunities to excel!

www.ingramcontent.com/pod-product-compliance
Lightning Source LLC
LaVergne TN
LVHW022259060326
832902LV00020B/3164